NEW
and
OLD
Voices
of

WAH'KON-TAH

Edited by Robert K. Dodge and Joseph B. McCullough
With a foreword by Vine Deloria, Jr.

INTERNATIONAL PUBLISHERS
New York

Copyright Acknowledgements

The poems in this book are copyrighted by the authors, or their publishers, or representatives who have graciously given their permission for use here. None of these poems may be reprinted without permission except by reviewers quoting passages in reviews. The biographical notes are also included in this copyright notice.

In addition to the poets who have given their permission to reprint their poems, the publishers are grateful for the specific permissions granted by the following institutions and publications: *The Institute of American Indian Arts*, A Bureau of Indian Affairs School, Santa Fe, N.M. for the poems of Harold Bird, Ramona Carden, Grey Cahoe, Phil George, Bruce Ignacio, King D. Kuka, Carles C. Long, Alonzo Lopez, David Martinez, Calvin O'John, Agnes Pratt, Ronald Rogers, Loyal Shegonee, Liz Sohappy, Soge Track, and Donna Whitewing; The *Mustang Review* for the poems of Fred Red Cloud; *Pembroke Magazine* for those of Ray Young Bear; the *South Dakota Review* for the poems of Paula Gunn Allen, Martha Chosa, Grey Cahoe, Patty Harjo, Bruce Ignacio, Alonzo Lopez, Emerson Blackhorse Mitchell, Simon Ortiz, Norman Russell, Loyal Shegonee, Liz Sohappy, Soge Track, Winifred Fields Walters, Archie Washburn, and James Welch; Malki Museum Press for Wendy Rose's "I Expected My Skin and Blood to Ripen"; The University of Illinois Press for Jim Barnes' poems; Thunder's Mouth Press for Joy Harjo's "The Woman Hanging from the Thirteenth Floor Window"; *Puerto Del Sol* for Joy Harjo's "Are You Still There"; and Holy Cow! Press for the poems of Roberta Hill Whiteman. Duane Niatum's "The Owl in the Rearview Mirror" and "Song from the Totem Maker" were published in an earlier form in *Digging Out the Roots*, Harper & Row, 1977; "The Waterfall Song" was published in *The Mahlahat Review*, No. 60, 1981.

Library of Congress Cataloging-in-Publication Data
Main entry under title:
New and old voices of Wah'kon-tah.
    1. American poetry—Indian authors.   2. American
poetry—20th century.
PS591.I55N4   1985   811'.54'080897   85-14445
ISBN 0-7178-0630-8
ISBN 0-7178-0629-4 (pbk.)

Printed in the USA

Wah'Kon-Tah is the "Great Mystery," the sum total of all things, the conception of an impersonal, spiritual and life-giving power. The Dakotas believe that there are two kinds of songs: songs made by people, and songs that come in visions through the spirits of *Wah'Kon-Tah*. It is from the voices of *Wah'Kon-Tah* that people gain spiritual power and wisdom.

There are many other names among the various Indian peoples—Wakonda, Wakan-tanka, Nesaru, Manito—that signify the same meaning as *Wah'Kon-Tah*.

Acknowledgements

Any anthology such as this one could not be compiled without the assistance of a number of people who rarely receive the credit they deserve. We are especially thankful to the following: to Mrs. T.D. Allen, for permission to use much of the material and for her generous help in supplying biographical information of many of the poets; to John R. Milton, editor of *The South Dakota Review*, for his permission to use material and for supplying addresses of some of the poets; and to Vine Deloria, Jr. for writing the provocative foreword to this book.

For this edition we would also like to express our thanks to Joseph Bruchac, editor of *The Greenfield Review*, for his valuable advice; to Annette Irwin of Interlibrary Loan Services at James R. Dickinson Library at the University of Nevada, Las Vegas; to our wives, Leslie Dodge and Judy Gerhart-McCullough; and, of course, to all the poets whose works form the contents.

R.D., J.M.
June, 1985

CONTENTS

Foreword

American Indians have been denied the chance to pass through the decades of history as an experiencing community of souls capable of transforming themselves into the possibilities which confront them. The Indians of today, the intrepid spirits who captured Alcatraz and defied the greatest military power on earth at Wounded Knee, remain as ghosts with little or no immediate identity, hidden in the shadows of the past. As they gather for a final stand the clouds of warriors past, Chief Joseph, Crazy Horse, Sitting Bull, Geronimo, Dull Knife, blot them out from the hundreds of anthologies that gallop past in the noon sun of popularity.

Denied the inherent right of national existence, American Indians can only do what the forgotten peoples of the past have done and preserve in song and poetry the suffering and strife of their existence. It is thus that we have this book, this effort to grasp from the fantasy-land of the white man's mind, a sense of historical being. In the poetry of the modern Indian we find a raging sense of having been and a desperate pronouncement of future being, an effort beyond nobility that calls for recognition of the humanity and nationality of Indian existence. In poetry the broken treaties and countless betrayals are overcome and the twisting coils of the law are transcended so that if there is to be no tangible existence there will be spiritual existence.

Indian poetry, like Indian art, has struggled to emerge from the stereotypes imposed on it by non-Indians who wished to see the simple and childish recitations and drawings of a creature not yet civilized but containing that possibility. The poetry of this book is not that taught in the schools and does not follow the patterns of formal existence. It is no more and no less than what would have naturally emerged from the experience of Indian existence had there been no white man to confront. It is awareness tempered with reflection and the holiness of history as it has been experienced.

Indian poetry may not say the things that poetry says because it does not emerge from the centuries of formal western thought. It is not, one can easily discern, descriptive. It has no formula for living. It is hardly chronological and its sequences relate to the integrity of the circle, not the directional determination of the line. It encompasses, it does not point.

One faces, in fact, a desperation in presenting a foreword to any book of Indian poetry because of the experiences of the past. The white man, it seems, refuses to make that final transition from his European past and to confront the continent and its people. He rather extracts what he feels is not harmful to himself or what can be profitably used, and hurriedly passes on, unable to lay down roots, unable to reflect, and most tragically of all, unable to savor experiences.

It is with great and tragic pleasure, therefore, that I write a foreword to this book. My greatest fear is that it will be taken as books on Indians by Indians are taken—as "quaint." Within this poetry by the best of the young Indian poets is contained a fearful effort to bridge the gap between Chief Joseph and Russell Means, the leader of the Wounded Knee protest. It is a lyrical attempt to provide a transition between the glorious past with which we all agree and the desperate present which Indians know and which the white man refuses to admit. Our poets are the only ones today who can provide this bridge, this reflective statement of what it means and has meant to live in a present which is continually overwhelmed by the fantasies of others of the meaning of past events.

No essay, no slogan, no policy, no pronouncement can rescue the American Indian from his banishment to the realms of mythology by the non-Indian. Only the poet in his frightful solitude and in his ability to transcend chronological existence can build that spiritual bridge which enables individuals to travel the roads of man's experiences. Thus while we struggle with the institutions and structures of modern life and the headlines run red with anger and frustration, it is only the poets who will tell us how the battle came to its conclusion.

With the poems of this book, then, the reader is invited to savor the Indian experience. It is only in savoring that the full integrity of experience is allowed to present itself. One should not gulp one's food for it is not for energy and vitamins alone that food is eaten. It is eaten as much for future remembrances and for this reason it is savored. Once savored this poetry may brush away the years and tell you more about the Indian's travels in historical experience than all the books written and lectures given. That may be the reason that poetry seems to survive where everything else expires. That may be why these Indians still sing their songs of poetry for us.

Vine Deloria, Jr.

Introduction

As much as any other racial or ethnic group, the American Indians have been the subject of stereotypes and myths that fail to perceive them in their real humanity. Deep seated prejudices and persecutions have been real dangers to their ability to survive as well as to their ability either to fully integrate into U.S. society or to preserve their own life style.

As perceived by white America the cultural image of the American Indian has been filtered through at least two important stereotypes or myths. One stereotype sees the Indian as a Noble Savage, the other as a red devil.

The stereotype of the Indian as a devil had its real beginning among the Puritans of Massachusetts, although there are foreshadowings of it in John Smith's account of Virginia, as there are also foreshadowings of the Noble Savage myth in Smith's portrayal of Pochahontas.

The Puritans saw their colonization of Massachusetts as a sacred mission. Standing in the way of that mission were dark savages who worshipped strange gods and who lived in the heart of dark forests, out of reach of the light of the sun as well as of the light of God's grace. The Puritans concluded that whatever stood in the way of their sacred mission was an obstacle set up by Satan, and that these dark men were agents of the devil. Seeing Indians at worship, the Puritans also decided that they were worshippers of Satan.

Such an image of the Indian allowed the Puritans to look upon the Pequod war, a war in which a combined force from Plymouth and Massachusetts Bay surrounded a camp of sleeping Indians, set fire to the dwellings, killed all they could (including women and children) during the battle, killed all the captive males over the age of adolescence after the battle, and enslaved everyone else, as a mark of God's special providence. After all, this was a battle against Satan and drastic measures were called for.

The myth of the Noble Savage, on the other hand, although foreshadowed in Smith's story of Pochahontas, did not come into full flower in America until the late eighteenth and early nineteenth centuries. It was a time of slowed westward expansion, the idea of Manifest Destiny had not yet taken hold of the American imagination and there was relatively little contact between whites and reds. When such contact did take place on the frontier, it led to events similar to the Pequod war, as a history of the Paxton Boys would show.

The Noble Savage myth began in Europe and spread to the cities and settled parts of America. Most of those who believed in it had seen few if any Indians.

It led to the spectacle of princes, historians, writers and others travelling to the plains to ride in the buffalo hunts and to observe the pure savage. The myth, of course, grew out of the romantic tradition, and perceived the Indian as one of the few uncorrupted humans then existing.

Today, these myths still exist, and still influence the perceptions of white Americans who observe American Indians. To some extent, these myths even affect the Indians' perceptions of themselves. For the readers of this book, it is important to realize that these two myths have their manifestations in white America's view of native American literature. Both myths tend to devalue the importance and the ability of native American writers.

Marlon Brando, most recently, has pointed out that we have all seen motion pictures in which the most intelligent comment made by an Indian (usually, of course, a white man pretending to be an Indian) was "Ugh!" Subtler directors or writers have more advanced Indians who are able to articulate more complex ideas such as "How?" and even "Me want firewater" and "That plenty right, *Kemo sabe*."

Such misconceptions of Indian speech are probably related to the myth of the Indian as a savage devil. Supposedly the Indians were "silent, sullen people incapable of articulate expression."[1]

However, according to Gerald W. Haslam, such misconceptions also result from the large differences between European and most Indian languages. Most Indian languages are agglutinative, and are pronounced relatively low and back in the mouth. The sounds, according to Haslam, have "a deep, throaty quality."[2]

It is easy to see, then, that to a European, a person speaking such a language would appear to be saying "Ugh," over and over, but it is important to remember that the languages of the American Indians are, in fact, capable of making the kind of distinctions that we expect of other languages.

At the other extreme, related to the myth of the Noble Savage, as well as to other misconceptions concerning Indian languages, is the belief that all American Indians are poetic. In *The Way*, Shirley Hill Witt and Stan Steiner demonstrate one of the results of this myth:

> A student at the Institute of American Indian Arts, in Santa Fe, New Mexico, was praised for his poetry. He objected: *In my tribe we have no poets. Everyone talks in poetry.* If poetry is the magical use of symbols and rhythm "to make life," as the Greeks defined it, or "to remake life," as the Cherokees say, his romanticism was realistic, at least in part. For in no segment of our society are poetry and song as religiously vital as among tribal traditionalists and modernists alike, as (the young Indian poets) attest.[3]

To be sure, in a tribal society there is a more intimate relationship between each person and the various functions of society, including the making of poetry, but to assert that everyone talks poetry is to deny what poetry really is. It is also to deny distinctions that American Indians make between poetry and prose.

A. Grove Day attempts to distinguish between Indian poetry and Indian prose.[4] Such a distinction suggests that Indians like whites do not always speak in poetry. To believe that they do diminishes the value of the poetry that they do write or chant. The writing of poetry, as Mrs. Terry Allen, long in charge of the creative writing department at the Institute of American Indian Arts, seems to have successfully taught many of her students, is a difficult task that involves the measuring of rhythms, the choice of words and symbols and the shaping of it all into a unity. It is a task that many Indian poets do well.

This is not to say that poetry does not play a large part in the everyday lives of many tribes. William Brandon points out that multivolume collections of ancient songs and chants "have been made from tiny Indian communities of only a few hundred persons."[5] Obviously, for such poems to have survived in an oral tradition within such small communities, they must have been considered important. Day points out that most of such songs and chants were religious in nature. "They attempted to get hold of the sources of supernatural power."[6]

There were special songs for baking bread, for chanting over a new baby or when making its cradle, for chanting while preparing to plant seed, to indicate only a few. Thus, the integration between religion, poetry and everyday life was great, but these songs still had been already composed, committed to memory and chanted as the occasion arose.

They were not made up, or talked, on demand. Thus, until the early 1970's, the two predominant attitudes toward American Indians had helped to make their poetry practically invisible to white America. Where such poetry had been observed, it had been largely the songs and chants that originated in a former day rather than the poetry of contemporary Indians.

Before the publication of the first edition of *Voices from Wah'Kon-Tah* three whites of some influence had helped in the development of a contemporary Indian poetry and in bringing that poetry to the attention of some white Americans. John Milton, editor of the *South Dakota Review*, had devoted two issues to the art and literature of contemporary American Indians, and Terry Allen had been director of the creative writing program at the Institute of American Indian Arts (IAIA) since 1963. Her students made up about half of the poets anthologized in the first edition. Brother Benet Tvedten, editor of *The Blue Cloud Quarterly*, had been publishing American Indian writers since 1967.

The poems that came out of the IAIA appeared to share the purpose of transforming the style of chants and songs into modern poetry, keeping in touch with their heritage through traditional forms. Such poets as Donna

Whitewing, Calvin O'John, Ronald Rogers, Emerson Blackhorse Mitchell and Phil George were represented in the first edition by poems that used forms derived from traditional chants and songs. They all achieved some degree of success in combining the ancient art form with the moderns. In this way Terry Allen's work at IAIA was rewarding.

The other poets represented in the first edition shared a concern for a connection with their Indian heritage, but most of the others let their subject matter show their heritage and drew their forms from the poetic forms of modern western poetry. The poems of James Welch, Simon Ortiz, Ray Young Bear, Fred Redcloud, Scott Momaday and others appeared more familiar to white readers for that reason. Yet, few of these poets had achieved any notice among white editors or readers, except for editors Brother Benet Tvedten and John Milton and their readers.

Since the Publication of *Voices from Wah'Kon-Tah* [1974], American Indian poetry has gathered its strength and is beginning to flourish. According to Andrew Wiget, more than one hundred books of Indian poetry have been published, mostly by small presses.[7] That is about four times as many as were published before our first edition.

Also, more editors of mainstream periodicals are beginning to publish Indian poets. To take one example, Roberta Hill Whiteman has published in *Poetry Northwest*, *The American Poetry Anthology*, *The Nation* and *The North American Review* as well as in other periodicals.

Carroll Arnett (Gogisgi) provides an example of another kind. Before 1974 Arnett had published five books of poetry and was establishing a reputation as an academic poet. His poems, however, did not appear to reflect his Indian heritage. There is, of course, no reason why a Cherokee poet has to write about Indian subjects, but in 1976 Arnett published *Tsalagi*, a book of poems that do reflect his Cherokee heritage. It was also about this time that he added the parenthetical (Gogisgi) to his name. Perhaps most important, since the publication of *Tsalagi*, we believe Arnett has strengthened an already strong poetic voice.

Today, many more poets are finding ways of expressing their Indian heritage in poetic forms, some by continuing to experiment with forms derived from chants and songs, and nearly all by finding poetic subjects derived from their Indian heritage.

We would like to think that *Voices from Wah'Kon-Tah* made some contribution to the changes that have taken place since its first publication, and, while it is probably true that *Voices* was a result of many of the same conditions that produced these changes, it is also true that it was the first anthology of Native American poetry that attempted to be comprehensive, and it may have been helpful in the strengthening of Native American poetry.

The poets added to this edition represent the best writers who have had time to become somewhat established. Other poets may soon become as important.

Like the poetry included in the first two editions, the added poems help to break down the stereotypical views of the American Indian. Those who wish to continue thinking of Indians in terms of racial stereotypes should not read their poetry. Those who wish to get to know Indians will find these poems provide a beginning, and getting to know someone is the surest way to beat down whatever stereotypes may have stood between you.

Finally, as Thomas Sanders and Walter Peek remind us, "to listen for the voice out of Wah'Kon-Tah that drifts through the English phrasings is to hear language enriched beyond spiritual bounds."[8]

Las Vegas, Nevada   ROBERT K. DODGE
August, 1985   JOSEPH B. McCULLOUGH

NOTES

[1]Gerald Haslam, ed. *Forgotten Pages of American Literature* (Boston, Houghton Mifflin, 1970), p. 14.

[2]Ibid., p. 15.

[3]Shirley Hill Witt and Stan Steiner (eds.) *The Way* (New York, Vintage, 1972), p. 132.

[4]A. Grove Day, *The Sky Clears* (Lincoln, Nebraska, University of Nebraska Press, 1970), p. 4.

[5]William Brandon, *The Magic World* (New York, Morrow, 1971), p. xi.

[6]Day, p. 6

[7]Andrew Wiget, "Sending a Voice: The Emergence of Contemporary Native American Poetry," *College English*, 46 (October, 1984), 598–609.

[8]Thomas E. Sanders and Walter W. Peek (eds.) *Literature of the American Indian* (New York, Glencoe Press, 1973), p. 449.

Voices
of
WAH' KON-TAH

Paula Gunn Allen

LAMENT OF MY FATHER, LAKOTA

O many-petaled light where
stands traitorous the sign of fall,
weave basket-symbols on the autumn skull of Old Coyote.[1]
Night no longer stays the hand of cause.
What innocence could now behold our days secure,
or light could move beyond the budding tears,
(woman sign that clings to eyes
no longer comforted by grief.)

Now come to us our broken victories,
hawks mounted on the tortured wings of kill;
old age sits upon the frozen window sills
too alien for our age-dimmed sight.
And fleshless fingers touch
the careful cobwebs of our days
that hold the butterfly called morning—
turned now into the owl song of night.

I have heard it said
that such poor creatures move in every land
and cast their shadow sign on every wintered skull.
Coyote and this night
be still.
I wonder how a man can cling to life.

[1] Coyote, the trickster-creator, who called himself the first man, is a frequent
figure in Indian mythology. According to one myth, the people discovered
that the Sun must be placated by human death, or he could not move. Coyote,
interpreter of signs, told the people that everyone must die. From this came
the belief that death would come quickly to those who glazed on the faces of
the dead.

Carroll Arnett

OUT IN THE WOODS

It must've been a dream.
I couldn't and still can't
believe the sonofabitch,
a sport, raised and
aimed a shotgun at me.

When his rifled slug
ripped the underbrush
on my left, my right
hand swung the lever,
arm set the bead, finger
squeezed a thump against
the shoulder to start
more thumps in the chest.

Scared shitless, I watched
him run like a true
madman for the road a
quarter mile off.

I couldn't and still can't
believe his jaunty red
hat lying in the thin
snow, the 150-grain
leaded crease in its
insulated crown.

Only one inch lower.
A sorry trophy.
He could be my brother.
It's not real.

THE STORY OF MY LIFE

Down there where I was
born and reared on

Oklahoma red dirt,

a whirling wind came
out of the east, took

me from the land

my grandfather drank
up, gambled away, land

he stole from the Cherokee

woman he married—an
only memory of her in her

near blindness scraping

the floral design on
her dinner plate—that wind

carried me all the way

to California to dive-bomb
cigarette butts, to fight

the Battle of Tijuana

whorehouses *semper*
fidelis, semper—another

dry wind took me

north to go drunk, go to
school, study long-range

genetic effects of driving

with a cold beer bottle
between one's legs, to think of

waking in the morning

knowing that's as good as
you're going to feel all

day long, knowing

the pure-dee truth of
a friend's saying,

A slave is anyone

who waits for someone
else to set him free—

took me north

to make a name (there stood
Jesus laughing to beat all,

saying, man, you sure

got your work cut out
for you)—sentenced to

upper midwestern land-

grant learneries by
way of Missouri at whose

World's fair Goyathlay

had signed autographs
for 10¢ apiece, being

allowed to keep half

for his own self—then
back east to Maine

where both the land and

those living on it are
too good to be true,

though progress throbs

all through the night—again
north among Ojibwe women

who still tell children,

"If ya don't be real real
good, Grandmother Spider'll

come down from Canada

and put medicine on ya."
Yet further on to Pig's Eye,

Minnesota, where at the

trials of Dennis and Russell
U.S. marshals wear

small green and yellow

diamond-shaped lapel pins
and get a hardon each

time the .357 Magnums

jounce snug against their
hips. Not wanting to

travel, I have traveled.

I have never been
a homeowner, have

always been a tenant,

will always be
a tenant and hold

as much as I can.

Liz Sohappy Bahe

ONCE AGAIN

Let go of the present and death.
Go to the place nearest the stars,
gather twigs, logs;
build a small fire,
a huge angry fire.

Gather nature's skin,
wet it, stretch it,
make a hard drum,
fill it with water
to muffle the sound.

THE PARADE

The light glows bright
as the parade begins.
Not everyone has come,
only the old ones.
The Eastern tribes came far,
dressed in cloth, wearing silver.
From the southeast trailed teared travelers
of the Five Civilized Tribes.
From the plains came buffalo hunters
dressed in beaded, fringed buckskin.
The light glows brighter
as each tribe passes.

It was such a long time ago
when he was first sighted,
running through the forest
like a frightened, swift lean deer.
When he danced in bird feathers,
dancing frenzied around blue ashes.
In the twilight of dawn, again he dances.
Drums thunder over creeks
to the swishing grasses on the plains.
Chants echo across the land of yellow maize,
along the paths of the sacred buffalo.

The years flow like running water.
Grasses grow yellow, rocks crumble to crust
as old ones come, they pass.

Charles G. Ballard

NAVAJO GIRL OF MANY FARMS

Navajo girl of Many Farms
You ride on blue wings
Why do you fear?
The drop of sun
Is but my hands
Resting at your door
The desert wind
Is but my voice
Saying you are slim
Saying you are strong
The morning light
Is but my song
Singing soft to you
Ride, ride away with me
On your bright, blue wings
We will never return
Navajo girl of Many Farms

YOU NORTHERN GIRL

You northern girl, be yet
The fine sand along the River Platte
Blue flames along hickory logs
Above the ground where dancers dance

South to the yellow world
The amber world of morning lakes
Long-stemmed stillness that seldom breaks
Nor disturbs the sun's resting place

Small birds have not the wings for this
The flight across time and unlocked rhythms
Nor are they as pebbles in a stream
With colors drawn deep from wintry days

You northern girl, speak yet
Of a time of many trees, many camps of the strong
Mountain peaks that guard the fertile land
The purer light now lost to man

Though in the furnace of the Southlands
Deep in the city's web we meet
We will wing our way to the River Platte
Toward the fires of our Indian world

THE MAN OF PROPERTY

Let's let the good man sign the bill
That deprived the Indian of his will
Let's build his house upon the hill
And bring to him our misery

His children will attend the finest school
His wife will live by the golden rule
His workers for him will play the fool
And take to him our misery

His name will be on the cornerstone
He will find it proper to loan
Proper to forget the ones who groan
And take to him our misery

His fences will stretch across the land
His constituents will clap and stand
The lights will burn along the strand
Far removed from our misery

But then will come a certain day
Brothers will link arms along the way
The raging night will come to stay
And he will know our misery

DURING THE PAGEANT AT MEDICINE LODGE

During the pageant at Medicine Lodge
One bright line this—recollected but passing away,
    like a leaf that escaped the fire; it
    appears still golden, life-inhabited,
    imbued with light, with the filtered hush
    of deep forests.

During the pageant at Medicine Lodge
Later it seemed that the redman had been only a dream
    on paper, an elegant falsehood strutting
    before pioneers, a dancing image fading
    deeper into the forests, into the wild streams,
    into earth itself. They were never real!
    They sang—bird-like, bear-like, like wind,
    rustle of trees, crickets—and were no more.

During the pageant at Medicine Lodge
Conversational scraps and ideas. "A few might have
    survived," I said. I wanted to say,
    "You and I." But why stab at thin air.
    The past survives in the mind. On that
    particular day in southern Kansas *no Indians*
    were there. It was a jolly ride, it was dusty
    and hot, it was fun, but the Indians,
    whoever they were, did not arrive.

CHANGING OF THE GUARD

Why do you hold the flag so high
Old fellow of the Sac and Fox?
Those stars were never in your sky

From times past we have gone to war
Now the young are speaking new words
So be it. They have done so before

And it must come to them, the flag
If they take it from these useless hands
It must still be there, high up and strong

Grandfather, or whatever you are
You have spoken your sold-out words
To your strength I cannot reply

I know only that the time has come
When gratitude for treachery is gone
When kisses for the greedy are unclean

When I take the flag, old man
It will be but to honor the forgotten dead
Those who died for the Indian dream

Let no more be said, my son
On this matter we are of one mind
In my old time way I pass it on to you

TIME WAS THE TRAIL WENT DEEP

Time was the trail went deep
From the granite ledge of the Verdigris
On west to rivers flat
And a rolling sea of grass

We followed the Arkansas to New Town
Of the Creeks and veered off
To low hills in the north
Where we camped in those final days

Having walked to never look back
Having talked to carry through
We disbanded and were no more
To choose finally is the Indian way

But time was the trail went deep
Into a green and vibrant land

NOW THE PEOPLE HAVE THE LIGHT

Now the people have the light
But time must pass, days of autumn
While the deer drink at the pool

Visions gathered by proud men
Will not affect the light, the summer rains
Must fall on a world of leaves

The swarms of small life on wings
Must find the lake, the evening birds
Bring back the songs of youth

Steaming riverbeds on the Great Plains
Must sigh for the lizard and receive
In dark sand the wayward stars

Mountain peaks high over the land
Must keep the watch through all the years
For now the people have the light

Jim Barnes

CONTEMPORARY NATIVE AMERICAN POETRY

For one thing, you can believe it:
the skin chewed soft enough to wear,
the bones hewn hard as a totem
from hemlock. It's a kind of scare-

crow that will follow you home nights.
You've seen it ragged against a field,
but you seldom think, at the time,
to get there it had to walk through hell.

AUTOBIOGRAPHICAL FLASHBACK: PUMA AND POKEWEED

I've spoken of home before and spotted crows
older than my hair. I generalize: home
is where hard is. And know it true. The crow
is constant color: his caw can crack a stone.

You keep your crows alive as best you can:
you remember a puma and pokeweed and trees
quick with wings and wind, tell yourself the fear
you felt along your fingertips would freeze

your sanity now, if you were child again,
free to feel again leaves upon your head,
to break off shoots of poke for suppertime,
to dream the cry of a puma one time heard.

Your memory is rocked by things you have
neglected; your stoned eyes are hard with world
you are late to see. And even now you know
the facts are wrong, as random and whorled

as fingerprints on records you've tried to keep
or the circling crows that blot your inland sky.

THE CHICAGO ODYSSEY

Looking north you try to break through the sky
with your bad eyes. You want to map the town.
The lake and leaden sky are one, a blank
canvas on which you'd like to sketch a face.
The artist in you tells you to wait for dream.
You wait and nothing comes. You try museums,
their rigid worth, view mummies and other
wonders hardly half as strange as this place,
this time. A gauze of snow spirals up your spine.
You tell yourself the ice age now begins
and you alone must escape to tell the tale:
the horror of his and hers fleshed in frost,
the scream caught suddenly in mid-flight,
the running child quick-frozen in the park,
towers icicled in reverse, the el turned
easy slope for otters.

                        All as the world turns
the other way. You turn and traffic whirs.
The astronomy is wrong: there are no stars,
moon breaks crystalline, the only zodiac
is flake on flake, a kaleidoscope of air.
You swore you'd know this town and now you don't.
Something has tipped the day and up is down;
you're trying your best to leave while there's still
a time. From each corner comes a siren's song.
Every street's a cliff you tack away from,
cotton in your ears against the damning wind
you never thought could be so cold, so insistent
on its icy trade, that barter would mean
the loss of teeth. You'll suck your eyes back in
your head, lean hard into the coming night.
lie always, go native, and by God survive.

Peter Blue Cloud

SWEETGRASS

Sweet rains of summer
remembered in wintertime
in drying sweetgrass.

The fragrance is a sweet warmth
as soft as a blossom's promise
as I early morning huddle
by the woodstove dreaming,
berries ripe there were
scattered in their seasons
on tree and bush and nesting
in grasses tall, waving,
calling in scented voice
to pleasure the day, to dream
undisturbed by outward signs
of traffic or throngs scuttling
to frantic destinations.
And pulling gently, one by one
the long whispers of grass
and hearing frog song and
watching a cattail bending
to the weight of a light question
a red-wing blackbird asks
observing the brilliant passage
of a silent snake, or
the dipping, turning swift
hunger in a swallow's flight.

I add a piece of wood
to the singing of the stove
and drift my mind to feel
again the hot sun on shoulders
the sweat on brow, the rich
feel of fertile soil I sink to
upon my knees resting
gathering with mind's fingers
a meadow of grasses
a hillside of forest
a clear brook curving
and widening to reflect
a white roundness of cloud.
    I curve my mind to rhythms
touched and tasted back then
here on winter's shelf
I sort memories and moods
and dwell on yesterday
and all because my body
brushed, in passing,
the bunches of sweetgrass
hanging in winter's house.

Joseph Bruchac

CANTICLE

Let others speak
of harps and
heavenly choirs
I've made my decision
to remain here
with the Earth

if the old grey poet
felt he could turn and
live with the animals
why should I be too good
to stay and die with them

and the great road of the Milky Way,
that Sky Trail my Abnaki ancestors
strode to the last Happy Home
does not answer my dreams

I do not believe
we go up to the sky
unless it is
to fall again
with the rain

NOT A THING OF PAINT OR FEATHERS

It was said by the Reverend
William Beauchamp that the way
of Handsome Lake, in his day,
was fast dying out
and that was in 1907.

And Arthur Parker,
whose father was Seneca,
told of the grief
of an Onondaga Teller of the Gai'wiio
over the passing of the old way
and that was in 1913.

And each of those who have written
of the Iroquois have clearly seen
that those old people
who knew the chants, the medicines,
the songs, the stories
have been growing fewer.

Yet the songs grow stronger
each Midwinter and those who come
to the Longhouses to hear
The Good Message
know that their belief
is not a thing of paint or feathers
but of the heart.

FROM AN INMATE RULE BOOK

Know your number
and cell location
if you forget
look in the mirror
and read them
in your eyes

when you have eaten
drop your spoon
into the bucket
beside the door
there are no knives
allowed in here
aside from those
in the Captain's smile

walk near the walls
they are the only
friends you can
always depend upon
to guard your back

wash as often
as they allow
try to convince
yourself the water
which falls
from the showerhead
is not some
invisible indelible paint
to mark you for
the rest of your life

Barney Bush

LEAVING OKLAHOMA AGAIN

for the
Creek Comet
Joy

wishing I had hitchiked
instead of busing it   thinking
about Joy back in
Oklahoma City   that we are
real close   closer than
brother and sister   closer than
lovers
closer than just being tribal
people   close as bones in
the earth
Part of it is this night
      leaving
already through Tulsa and
watching the halfmoon dip into
an Oklahoma horizon   how we ve
both seen it before   through
greyhound windows   airplanes
trains   and in its perfect
angle from the roadside
thumbing

Buses are americas last
stagecoaches   the saddest
farewells   last escapes from
boyfriends   girlfriends
army posts   parents   isolation
Abandoned elders leave yankee
winters

sometimes trailing renegade
children to Florida   or
Phoenix   to cramped trailer homes
Inside the bus there is only
arctic winter or sahara summer
incredible body stench   and
kids crying all night   and
the little blond kid   that
bus companies must hire to
squirm its ungendered body through
the seats onto my lap and
notebook   Juan always
smiles from across the aisle
passing me his brown paper bag
which I never refuse
Tequila was made for
bus trips   so are bolo ties
and plastic turquoise
Two 95 for a hamburger   no
refills on coffee   the bus
station gestapo gruffly informs
as if we had just arrived from
skidrow on our way to Dachau
The little blond kid always
has a mother   who comes from the
bathroom   fresh fragrant
not a hair out of place
smiling serenely as her kid plops
its yet dirty face and unkept
body on the stool next to mine
Momma smiles again   for me to
acknowledge her reshuffled deck
I smile back sadly   everytime
feeling my tequila and
leaving Oklahoma again.

Ramona Carden

THE MOCCASINS OF AN OLD MAN

I hung you there, moccasins of worn buckskin.
I hung you there and there you are still.
I took you from the hot flesh of a swift buck.
I took you to my woman.

She tanned you with buck brains.
She cut and sewed and beaded.
I wore you with pride.
I wore you with leaping steps over many grounds.

Now, I sit here and my bones are stiff with many winters.
You hang there and I shall sit.
We shall watch the night approach.

TUMBLEWEED

I stood in the shelter of a great tree,
Hiding from the wind that galloped over the land.
Robbing, and wrecking, and scattering. It soared.
I was earth bound.
It tugged at the leaves,
At the grass, at things not tied.
At me.
Urging, pulling, laughing in my ear.
I listened but stood.
Flitting away, it spied a tumbleweed
and coaxed it from its roots.
The brown weed soared
and became part of the wind.
Suddenly, with a wild yearning,
I ran stumbling, with arms outstretched.
It flew on beyond me.
It stopped.
The wind flew around me,
Leaving me there.

Martha Chosa

DRUMS

Throbbing—all I can hear!
Why can't there be bells,
with floating voices
over all our dry land?
Is it going to rain?
Or is that my people
need to dance more often?
Perhaps the Sky
is watching us with anger.
Are people talking behind his back?
Suppose he's sad
of not having enough power
to drop blessing on the land,
on my people,
on my crops,
on my animals?
People! People! People!
Brothers and sisters!
Let us give pride to the Sky;
help him to send
blessing for our needs.
Leave your drums.
Let him be proud of his powers.
Great Spirit!
Now is the time to have joy.

Great Sky!
It is time to see drops
of rain and of blessing
on our dry land.

Grey Cohoe

THE FOLDING FAN

The wild beauty of an eagle, once born to virgin sky
   now held in a sacred fan.
                           Beaded feathers
stiffen the grasp, the fingers that curled
to ease the cold soul but let the agony tear,
   for the heart will weep all the same.
Never again is life made vivid
   or for who else the kind warmth?
Maybe this I know, that it is for the dying,
whose ending breaths I hear not, as the wisdom
                        will come no more,
   only to grave, olden with age.
Eternity flies now on the wings of the gone soul,
                       never to be seen.
   Listen,
a drum I hear, distance, yet;
        it's from the folding fan.
                The preying bird of death is waiting,
                         calling.

Anita Endrezze-Danielson

SHAMAN/BEAR

He sniffs the autumn air,
fur bristling, rippling, like a red robe
of falling leaves. He looks for me.
I am a tamarack this time
my fingers yellow as meadow
grass changing in the light:
now thick with pine-dark dew,
now frost black as his snout. He rises
pawing stumps slashed by lightning
before I was born. He remembers
the hard heat splitting the air
clouds deep in his throat summers ago
the sun smoking in a tree.
Now he eats ashes, making spells
in a tongue few Indians speak.

He knows I'm here, legs trembling, cheeks red
as kinnikinic berries. It is time.
The Moon of Popping Trees has darkened
the gold birches. I dream of the season
His spell will cause my belly to swell
child heavy my womb full
as a Salmonberry moon.

Louise Erdrich

JACKLIGHT

The same Chippewa word is used both for flirting and hunting game,
while another Chippewa word connotes both using force in intercourse
and also killing a bear with one's bare hands.

—R. W. Dunning
(1959) *Social and Economic Change Among the Northern Ojibwa*

We have come to the edge of the woods,
out of brown grass where we slept, unseen,
out of knotted twigs, out of leaves creaked shut,
out of hiding.

At first the light wavered, glancing over us.
Then it clenched to a fist of light that pointed,
searched out, divided us.
Each took the beams like direct blows the heart answers.
Each of us moved forward alone.

We have come to the edge of the woods,
drawn out of ourselves by this night sun,
this battery of polarized acids,
that outshines the moon.

We smell them behind it
but they are faceless, invisible.
We smell the raw steel of their gun barrels,
mink oil on leather, their tongues of sour barley.
We smell their mothers buried chin-deep in wet dirt.
We smell their fathers with scoured knuckles
teeth cracked from hot marrow.
We smell their sisters of crushed dogwood, bruised apples,
of fractured cups and concussions of burnt hooks.

We smell their breath steaming lightly behind the jacklight.
We smell the itch underneath the caked guts on their clothes.
We smell their minds like silver hammers
cocked back, held in readiness
for the first of us to step into the open.

We have come to the edge of the woods,
out of brown grass where we slept, unseen,
out of leaves creaked shut, out of our hiding.
We have come here too long.

It is their turn now,
their turn to follow us. Listen,
they put down their equipment.
It is useless in the tall brush.
And now they take the first steps, not knowing
how deep the woods are and lightless.
How deep the woods are.

THE STRANGE PEOPLE

The antelope are strange people . . . they are beautiful to look at, and yet they are tricky. We do not trust them. They appear and disappear; they are like shadows on the plains. Because of their great beauty, young men sometimes follow the antelope and are lost forever. Even if those foolish ones find themselves and return, they are never again right in their heads.

—*Pretty Shield, Medicine Woman of the Crows,*
transcribed and edited by Frank Linderman (1932)

All night I am the doe, breathing
his name in a frozen field,
the small mist of the word
drifting always before me
.
And again he has heard it
and I have gone burning
to meet him, the jacklight
fills my eyes with blue fire;
the heart in my chest
explodes like a hot stone.

Then slung like a sack
in the back of his pickup,
I wipe the death scum
from my mouth, sit up laughing,
and shriek in my speeding grave.

Safely shut in the garage,
when he sharpens his knife
and thinks to have me, like that,
I come toward him,
a lean gray witch,
through the bullets that enter and dissolve.

I sit in his house
drinking coffee till dawn,
and leave as frost reddens on hubcaps,
crawling back into my shadowy body.
All day, asleep in clean grasses,
I dream of the one who could really wound me.

THE LADY IN THE PINK MUSTANG

The sun goes down for hours, taking more of her along
than the night leaves her with.
A body moving in the dust
must shed its heavy parts in order to go on.

Perhaps you have heard of her, the Lady in the Pink Mustang,
whose bare lap is floodlit from under the dash,
who cruises beneath the high snouts of semis, reading
the blink of their lights. *Yes, Move Over. Now.*
or *How Much*. Her price shrinks into the dark.

She can't keep much trash in a Mustang,
and that's what she likes. Travel light. Don't keep
what does not have immediate uses. The road thinks ahead.
It thinks for her, a streamer from Bismarck to Fargo
bending through Minnesota to accommodate the land.

She won't carry things she can't use anymore.
Just a suit, sets of underwear, what you would expect
in a Pink Mustang. Things she could leave anywhere.

There is a point in the distance where the road meets itself,
where coming and going must kiss into one.
She is always at the place, seen from behind,
motionless, torn forward, living in a zone
all her own. It is like she has burned right through time,
the brand, the mark, owning the woman who bears it.

She owns them, not one will admit what they cannot
come close to must own them. She takes them along,
traveling light. It is what she must face every time
she is touched. The body disposable as cups.

To live, instead of turn, on a dime.
One light point that is so down in value
Painting her nipples silver for a show, she is thinking
You out there. What do you know.

Come out of the dark where you're safe. Kissing these
bits of change, stamped out, ground to a luster,
is to kiss yourself away piece by piece
until we're even. Until the last
coin is rubbed for luck and spent.
I don't sell for nothing less.

Phil George

OLD MAN, THE SWEAT LODGE[1]

"This small lodge is now
The womb of our mother, Earth,
This blackness in which we sit,
The ignorance of our impure minds.
These burning stones are
The coming of new life."
I keep his words near my heart.

Confessing, I recall my evil deeds.
For each sin, I sprinkle water on fire-hot stones,
The hissed steam is sign that
The place from which Earth's seeds grow
Is still alive,
He sweats,
I sweat.

I remember, Old Man heals the sick,
Brings good fortune to one deserving.
Sacred steam rises;
I feel my pores give out their dross.
After I chant prayers to the Great Spirit,
I raise the door to the East.
Through this door dawns wisdom.

[1] The sweat lodge was almost universal for all tribes north of Mexico. It was usually a small round house made of sod, sticks or hide; an individual entered and hot rocks and water were placed inside to cause steam. After remaining for a time, he would then plunge into snow or cold water. The sweat lodge was used for religious purposes, to purify oneself as well as to cure disease. Special rituals were also conducted there.

Cleansed, I dive into icy waters.
Pure, I wash away all of yesterday.
"My son, Walk in this new life.
It is given to you!
Think right, feel right,
Be happy."
I thank you, Old Man, the Sweat Lodge.

ASK THE MOUNTAINS

Here I stand
For centuries watching
Moccasined trails
Wear down into
Paved highways.
Innumerable winter snows
Have robed me and
My sister—
Mother Earth.
To this moist
Green valley,
The Land of Winding Waters—
I give the beauty of
Purple peaks pointing.
From long ago
I have towered—
Unafraid.

Guarding ancient
Bits of wisdom
Learned by men and creatures.
To all inhabitants of this
New Switzerland,
The Mighty One
Smiles sunshine—
Together in happiness
We protect, provide.
In gaiety, liberty,
I saw the Nez Perce
Freely worship.
Pure as my
Glacial Waters,
Proud as the bull Elk
They lived—
Seeking to survive
Within my shadow.
I helped establish these
Intelligent, ritualistic
People—a powerful race.
I admire their
Love for life.
From tribal burial grounds,
I have seen
Peace die and
Violence invade,
I know all truth.
I am Wallowa of the
Blue Mountains.

NIGHT BLESSING

Sleep plays hide-and-seek with darkness.
In reverence
All earth stands, head bowed.
Long-needled evergreens cease to
Proclaim hushed hymns of awe.
Between praise stanzas,
Night birds pause to listen,
While sending their magnetic fragrance,
The sweetness for this royalty,
Spring flowers in carpet hues
Halt their prancing dance.
Stars shoot through space
To herald Full Moon's entrance.

Within my tepee
I cannot remain on robes and blankets.
Far out into the still of night,
My heart goes forth.
I must stand in honor, respect,
One beside a tepee shadows
Gazing toward snow-capped mountains.
I turn to face the East,
Waiting to receive
Her blessing.
"Oh, Ruler of the Night,
May I so live that all I do in time
Is preparation for lasting peace."

Soon Dawn's mystic gaze
Moves toward me,
Falling upon each creature.
I raise yeaming arms
And stand naked

Within Her sacred view.
Devotion surges in me
Overflows my littleness
And I must praise
In song and dance.
I am clothed in joy.
1 am warmed, protected.
Content, I sleep.

BATTLE WON IS LOST

They said, "You are no longer a lad."
    I nodded.
They said, "Enter the council lodge."
    I sat.
They said, "Our lands are at stake."
    I scowled.
They said, "We are at war."
    I hated.
They said, "Prepare red war symbols."
    I painted.
They said, "Count coups."
    I cringed.
They said, "Desperate warriors fight best."
    I charged.
They said, "Some will be wounded."
    I bled.
They said, "To die is glorious."
    They lied.

Janet Campbell Hale

TRIBAL CEMETERY

I lay my hand
Upon
The coldness of the smooth
White stone,
My fingers touch the words,
I read again:
My father's name,
Date of birth,
Date of death,
Veteran of
World War I.

"This is your
Grandfather's grave,"
I tell my children,
Wishing I could tell them,
That they would understand,
That the man
Who was my father,
Was of that first generation,
Born on old land
Newly made reservation,
That at twelve,
He went to Mission School,
To learn to wear shoes,
To eat with knife and fork,
To pray to the Catholic God,
To painfully
Learn English words,
English meanings,
White ways of thinking,

English words,
To speak,
To think,
To write,
English words,
When we,
My children
And I
Know no others.

I lay my hand
Upon
The cold white
Stone,
My daughter,
Who is four,
Gathers small rocks,
With which she
Fills her pockets,
She sings to herself
As she goes along.

My son,
Who is ten,
Stays with me awhile,
Beside my father's grave,
asks me about my
Childhood,
About the others,
Lying buried here,
In Campbell-labeled
graves.
Then he leaves me,
And goes about
The cemetery,
Reading tombstones,
For unusual names,
Looking for people,
Who lived
One-hundred years,
Or more—
He's found five.

Joy Harjo

THE WOMAN HANGING FROM THE THIRTEENTH FLOOR WINDOW

She is the woman hanging from the 13th floor
window. Her hands are pressed white against the
concrete moulding of the tenement building. She
hangs from the 13th floor window in east Chicago,
with a swirl of birds over her head. They could
be a halo, or a storm of glass waiting to crush her.

She thinks she will be set free.

The woman hanging from the 13th floor window
on the east side of Chicago is not alone.
She is a woman of children, of the baby, Carlos,
and of Margaret, and of Jimmy who is the oldest.
She is her mother's daughter and her father's son.
She is several pieces between the two husbands
she has had. She is all the women of the apartment
building who stand watching her, watching themselves.

When she was young she ate wild rice on scraped down
plates in warm wood rooms. It was in the farther
north and she was the baby then. They rocked her.

She sees Lake Michigan lapping at the shores of
herself. It is a dizzy hold of water and the rich
live in tall glass houses at the edge of it. In some
places Lake Michigan speaks softly, here, it just sputters
and butts itself against the asphalt. She sees
other buildings just like hers. She sees other
women hanging from many-floored windows
counting their lives in the palms of their hands
and in the palms of their children's hands.

She is the woman hanging from the 13th floor window
on the Indian side of town. Her belly is soft from
her children's births, her worn levis swing down below
her waist, and then her feet, and her heart.
She is dangling.

The woman hanging from the 13th floor hears voices.
They come to her in the night when the lights have gone
dim. Sometimes they are little cats mewing and scratching
at the door, sometimes they are her grandmother's voice,
and sometimes they are gigantic men of light whispering
to her to get up, to get up, to get up. That's when she wants
to have another child to hold onto in the night, to be able
to fall back into dreams.

And the woman hanging from the 13th floor window
hears other voices. Some of them scream out from below
for her to jump, they would push her over. Others cry softly
from the sidewalks, pull their children up like flowers and gather
them into their arms. They would help her, like themselves.

But she is the woman hanging from the 13th floor window,
and she knows she is hanging by her own fingers, her
own skin, her own thread of indecision.

She thinks of Carlos, of Margaret, of Jimmy.
She thinks of her father, and of her mother.
She thinks of all the women she has been, of all
the men. She thinks of the color of her skin, and
of Chicago streets, and of waterfalls and pines.
She thinks of moonlight nights, and of cool spring storms.
Her mind chatters like neon and northside bars.
She thinks of the 4 a.m. lonelinesses that have folded
her up like death, discordant, without logical and
beautiful conclusion. Her teeth break off at the edges.
She would speak.

The woman hangs from the 13th floor window crying for
the lost beauty of her own life. She sees the
sun falling west over the grey plane of Chicago.
She thinks she remembers listening to her own life
break loose, as she falls from the 13th floor
window on the east side of Chicago, or as she
climbs back up to claim herself again.

"ARE YOU STILL THERE"

there are sixty-five miles
of telephone wire
between acoma
                and albuquerque
i dial the number
and listen for the sound
of his low voice
                on the other side
"hello"
          is a gentle motion of a western wind
cradling tiny purple flowers
that grow near the road
                towards laguna
i smell them
as i near the rio puerco bridge
my voice stumbles
returning over sandstone
         as it passes the cañocito exit

Patty Harjo

MUSINGS

Walk proud, walk straight, let your thoughts race
with the blue wind, but do not bare your soul to
your enemies.

The black mountain lion called night devours the
white rabbit of day. And the icy wind blows
over the still-warm, brown earth.

In restless dreams I called out his name,
Waking, I do not remember.

In my score of years
I have known not love
except wind, earth and darkness.

Lance Henson

WARRIOR NATION TRILOGY

1
from the mountains we come
lifting our voices for the beautiful
road you have given

we are the buffalo people
we dwell in the light of our father sun
in the shadow of our mother earth

we are the beautiful people
we roam the great plans without fear
in our days the land has taught us oneness
we alone breathe with the rivers
we alone hear the song of the stones

2
oh ghost that follows me
find in me strength to know the wisdom
of this life

take me to the mountain of my grandfather
i have heard him all night
singing among the summer leaves

3

great spirit (maheo)

make me whole
i have come this day with my spirit
i am not afraid
for i have seen in vision
the white buffalo
grazing the frozen field
which grows near the full circle
of this
world

EIGHT POEMS FOR AUGUST

face grown inward
a stone over which water
has passed many
years

climbing into evening
i am
bone
chipped
by
light

telling which way to go
         gaze of the
river

soft rain prints
         the earth into memory

crow out of early
darkness
asks
         who is
         left

against a grey sky
sparrows

pieces of us shiver
in their
light

each shadow is someone
dreaming

quiet as dew
down inside of a leaf
we raise up
again

Linda Hogan

CELEBRATION: BIRTH OF A COLT

When we reach the field
she is still eating
the heads of yellow flowers
and pollen has turned her whiskers
gold. Lady,
her stomach bulges out,
the ribs have grown wide.
We wait,
our bare feet dangling
in the horse trough,
warm water
where goldfish brush
our smooth ankles.
We wait
while the liquid breaks
down Lady's dark legs
and that slick wet colt
like a black tadpole
darts out
beginning at once
to sprout legs.
She licks it to its feet,
the membrane still there,
red,
transparent
the sun coming up shines through,
the sky turns bright with morning
and the land
with pollen blowing off the corn,
land that will always own us,
everywhere it is red.

Bruce Ignacio

LOST

I know not of my forefathers
nor of their beliefs
For I was brought up in the city.
Our home seemed smothered and surrounded
as were other homes on city sites.
When the rain came
I would slush my way to school
as though the street were a wading pool.
Those streets were always crowded.
I brushed by people with every step,
Covered my nose once in a while,
Gasping against the smell of perspiration on humid days.
Lights flashed everywhere
until my head became a signal, flashing on and off.
Noise so unbearable
I wish the whole place would come to a standstill,
leaving only peace and quiet

And still, would I like this kind of life? . . .
The life of my forefathers
who wandered, not knowing where they were going,
but just moving, further and further
from where they had been,
To be in quiet,
to kind of be lost in their dreams and wishing,
as I have been to this day,
I awake.

Maurice Kenny

WILD STRAWBERRY

For Helene

And I rode the Greyhound down to Brooklyn
where I sit now eating woody strawberries
grown on the backs of Mexican farmers
imported from the fields of their hands,
juices without color or sweetness

     my wild blood berries of spring meadows
     sucked by June bees and protected by hawks
     have stained my face and honeyed
     my tongue . . . healed the sorrow in my flesh

     vines crawl across the grassy floor
     of the north, scatter to the world
     seeking the light of the sun and innocent
     tap of the rain to feed the roots
     and bud small white flowers that in June
     will burst fruit and announce spring
     when wolf will drop winter fur
     and wrens will break the egg

     my blood, blood berries that brought laughter
     and the ache in the stooped back that vied
     with dandelions for the plucking,
     and the wines nourished our youth and heralded
     iris, corn and summer melon

we fought bluebirds for the seeds
armed against garter snakes, field mice;
won the battle with the burning sun
which blinded our eyes and froze our hands
to the vines and the earth where knees knelt
and we laughed in the morning dew like worms
and grubs; we scented age and wisdom

my mother wrapped the wounds of the world
with a sassafras poultice and we ate
wild berries with their juices running
down the roots of our mouths and our joy

I sit here in Brooklyn eating Mexican
berries which I did not pick, nor do
I know the hands which did, nor their stories . . .
January snow falls, listen . . .

CORN-PLANTER

I plant corn four years:
ravens steal it;
rain drowns it;
August burns it;
locusts ravage leaves.

I stand in a circle and throw seed.
Old men laugh because they know the wind
will carry the seed to my neighbor.

I stand in a circle on planted seed.
Moles burrow through the earth
and harvest my crop.

I throw seed to the wind
and wind drops it on the desert.

The eighth year I spend planting corn;
I tend my fields all season.
After September's harvest I take it to the market.
The people of my village are too poor to buy it.

The ninth spring I make chicken-feather headdresses,
plastic tom-toms and beaded belts.
I grow rich,
buy an old Ford,
drive to Chicago,
and get drunk
on Welfare checks.

King D. Kuka

"A TASTE OF HONEY"

True: nor love or loving is ultimate.
A doe, free in the valley,
    that but her head concealed by green,
    hoofs cleansed by artesian waters,
Is harnessed by love that shuns her.
While beauty slumbers, tonight love travels afar.

Love is nay but thatching in a storm,
    for a wind tears damp and cold,
    cruel and ruthless.
A fallen traveler like weather-beaten gaff
    shall sink, rise, sink, rise, thrice sink,
    rise ne'er from love experienced in icy depths.
The thickened lung is so with breath,
Not satisfaction of love.

Love is peace, yet it is mortal.
Plead release.
Console yourself with sorrow;
Tantalized you shall be by love.
Treasure love's memory.
Sell it to tears, regret, self-pity.
Love's outstretched arms seek to destroy you.

Love is the venom of a reptile;
A wasp, fitter to kill than keep.

Within the venom dwells death;
Without is honey.
Gamble carelessly venom's deadly game
    and you'll be dealt a losing hand.
Carefully give, and in return
Will be "a taste of honey."

Littlebird

DEATH IN THE WOODS

Corn swaying in the rhythm of the wind—
   Graceful ballerinas,
   Emerging at the edge of the forest.
All dip and dance;
   Wind tunnels through long silken hair,
   Golden teeth-seeds.
Trees chatter nervously
   Awakening sky in fright,
   Pointing at Woodman.
A mighty thud! Blow leaves deep scar;
   He strikes again . . .
Corn mourns, golden tears,
   Bows, praying for fallen brother.
Jay mocks the greedy beast
   Who has doomed majestic brother,
   His life home.
Wind tosses leaves aside as
   Woodman tramps on his way,
   Ax dripping oak's blood.
The forest, damp and silent,
   Mourning for lost Oak.
   And now remains but a
   Chirp of a lonely cricket and

   Silhouette of Woodman,
   Diminishing,
     beyond the
       saddened hill
         as the far
           sun sinks.

Charles C. Long

YEI-IE'S CHILD[1]

I am the child of the Yei-ie.
Turquoise for my body, silver for my soul,
I was united with beauty all around me.
As turquoise and silver, I'm the jewel
       of brother tribes and worn with pride.
The wilds of the animals are also my brothers.
The bears, the deer, and the birds are a part
       of me and I am a part of them.
As brothers, the clouds are our long, sleek hair.
The winds are our pure breath.
As brothers, the rivers are our blood.
The mountains are our own selves.
As brothers, the universe is our home and
       in it we walk
With beauty in our minds,
With beauty in our hearts, and
With beauty in our steps.
       In beauty we were born.
       In beauty we are living.
       In beauty we will die.
       In beauty we will be finished.

[1] Yei or Yeibichai is one of the most ancient of the Navajo gods. Like the gods of the ancient Greeks, they are conceived of as partly human.

Alonzo Lopez

DIRECTION

I was directed by my grandfather
To the East,
    so I might have the power of the bear;
To the South,
    so I might have the courage of the eagle;
To the West,
    so I might have the wisdom of the owl;
To the North,
    so I might have the craftiness of the fox;
To the Earth,
    so I might receive her fruit;
To the Sky,
    so I might lead a life of innocence.

I AM CRYING FROM THIRST

I am crying from thirst.
I am singing for rain.
I am dancing for rain.
The sky begins to weep,
        for it sees me
        singing and dancing
        on the dry, cracked
        earth.

THE LAVENDER KITTEN

Miles and miles of pasture
    rolled on before me.
Covered with grass and clover
    dyed pink, white, and blue.
At the edge of the fluctuating
    sea of watercolors
Sat a lavender kitten.
Its fur glinted from an oscillating
    ray of pink.
Quivered gently at the touch of a
    swirling blue breeze.
Its emerald eyes glittered
And gazed blindly at the lighting
    and fading sky of hazy red,
Yellow, white, and blue.
My heart knocked within my chest.
I must have the lavender kitten!
I ran across the multi-colored field,
    my arms reaching forward.
Time slowed.
I tried to run faster
    but moved twice as slowly.
The blue breeze circled and tightened
    around me,
Holding me back.
The kitten rose and stretched
    sending lavender mist
Swimming in every direction.
It turned and started away
    in huge, slow strides.

I followed and,
    by a shimmering prism lake,
I came within reach of the kitten.
I offered my hand
    and the kitten edged away,
Farther and farther.
The lake turned from crystal
    to deep purple.
I looked around.
The colors began to melt.
The red sun turned to dull gray.
The color-filled sky turned to black.
The grass and clover began
    to wither and die.
I looked down into the pool before me,
There, at the bottom of
    the orchid glass cage,
Lay the lavender kitten.

David W. Martinez

NEW WAY, OLD WAY

Beauty in the old way of life—
The dwellings they decorated so lovingly;
A drum, a clear voice singing,
And the sound of laughter.

You must want to learn from your mother,
You must listen to old men
    not quite capable of becoming white men.
The white man is not our father.
While we last, we must not die of hunger.
We were a very Indian, strong, competent people,
But the grass had almost stopped its growing,
The horses of our pride were near their end.

Indian cowboys and foremen handled Indian herds.
A cowboy's life appealed to them until economics and
    tradition clashed.
No one Indian was equipped to engineer the water's flow
    onto a man's allotment.
Another was helpless to unlock the gate.
The union between a hydro-electric plant and
Respect for the wisdom of the long-haired chiefs
Had to blend to build new enterprises
By Indian labor.

Those mighty animals graze once more
    upon the hillside.
At the Fair appear again our ancient costumes.
A full-blood broadcasts through a microphone
    planned tribal action.
Hope stirs in the tribe,
Drums beat and dancers, old and young, step forward.

We shall learn all these devices the white man has,
We shall handle his tools for ourselves.
We shall master his machinery, his inventions, his skills,
    his medicine, his planning;
But we'll retain our beauty
And still be Indians!

THIS IS TODAY

This is today,
Within walking distance of the waterhold,
Oil wells pump around the clock,
    and it is less than a day's drive
    to where factories build missiles
    and rockets and space-age hardware.
This is today
    but it has not yet come to those Navajos
    who take their domestic water
    from waterholes, and haul it
    in horse-drawn wagons
    to mud-walled hogans.
This is today.
It makes a beautiful picture
    Provided the viewer's water
    is piped into his home,
    and the vehicle that brings him
    to Navajo land
    is pulled by a three-hundred-horse-power
    engine.
This is today.
    but the Navajos are not to be pitied
They who drink the brown water
    and ride the wagons
    find beauty in this scene.
This is their wealth
This is today.

Emerson Blackhorse Mitchell

MIRACLE HILL

I stand upon my miracle hill,
　　Wondering of the yonder distance.
Thinking, When will I reach there?

I stand upon my miracle hill.
The wind whispers in my ear.
I hear the songs of old ones.

I stand upon my miracle hill.
　　My loneliness I wrap around me.
It is my striped blanket.

I stand upon my miracle hill
　　And send out touching wishes
To the world beyond hand's reach.

I stand upon my miracle hill.
　　The bluebird that flies above
Leads me to my friend, the white man.

I come again to my miracle hill.
　　At last, I know the all of me—
Out there, beyond, and here upon my hill.

THE NEW DIRECTION

This vanishing old road,
    Through hail-like dust storm,
It stings and scratches,
    Stuffy, I cannot breathe.

Here once walked my ancestors,
    I was told by the old ones,
One can dig at the very spot,
    And find forgotten implements.

Wasting no time I urged on,
    Where I'd stop I knew not,
Startled I listened to the wind,
    It whistled, screamed, cried,
"You! Go back, not this path!"

Then I recalled this trail
    Swept away by the north wind,
It wasn't for me to follow,
    The trail of the Long Walk.[1]

Deciding between two cultures,
    I gave a second thought,
Reluctantly I took the new one,
    The paved rainbow highway.

I had found a new direction.

---

[1] The Long Walk refers to one of the most tragic and pathetic episodes in the history of Anglo-Indian relations. Under the direction of General James Carleton and Colonel Christopher "Kit" Carson, the Navajo Indians of New Mexico were pursued, rounded up and driven to a wretched reservation on the banks of the Rio Pecos, in east-central New Mexico—the infamous Bosque Redondo.

THE PATH I MUST TRAVEL

Within the curved edge of quarter moon
    I was told there is a road
I must travel to meet the divine one,
    On this glittering crescent.

Awed, I tremble, enfolding tobacco
    The Almighty has given us,
To put forth our faith prayers
    Rolled in the precious smoke.

I wait in patience for the light,
    Gazing at glowing galaxies
Beyond the curve of risen silver bow.
    Silent, I sit listening.

Before me I see wrinkled old man,
    Torch in his right hand for me.
I breathe in burning leaf smoke.
    I hear waterdrum and a rattle.

Fasting through the long hours,
    I stand before the universe
I hold forth my hands four times,
    I see the Mighty One!

Within the whirling mist smoke,
    The drifting scent of cedar,
The fluffy eagle feather wakes me.
I step out into blinding space.

THE FOUR DIRECTIONS

A century and eight more years,
        Since Kit Carson rode from four directions,
Deep into the heart of nomadic Navahos,
        Burning, ravishing the Land of Enchantment.

Prairie grasses are once more
        Growing as high as the horse's belly.
Cradles of wrapped babies in colors
        Of the rainbow again span the land.

I know my people will stand and rise again.
        Now it is time.
Pollen of yellow grain,
        Scatter in the four directions.

N. Scott Momaday

THE BEAR

What ruse of vision
escarping the wall of leaves,
        rending incision
into countless surfaces,

        would cull and color
his somnolence, whose old age
        has outworn valor,
all but the fact of courage?

        Seen, he does not come,
move, but seems forever there,
        dimensionless, dumb,
in the windless noon's hot glare.

        More scarred than others
these years since the trap maimed him,
        pain slants his withers,
drawing up the crooked limb.

        Then he is gone, whole,
without urgency, from sight,
        as buzzards control,
imperceptibly, their flight.

ANGLE OF GEESE

How shall we adorn
Recognition with our speech?—
    Now the dead firstborn
Will lag in the wake of words.

    Custom intervenes;
    More than language means,
We are civil, something more:
The mute presence mulls and marks.

    Almost of a mind,
We take measure of the loss;
    I am slow to find
The mere margin of repose.

    And one November
It was no longer in the watch,
    As if forever,
Of the huge ancestral goose.

    So much symmetry!
Like the pale angle of time
    And eternity.
The great shape labored and fell.

    Quit of hope and hurt,
It held a motionless gaze,
    Wide of time, alert,
On the dark distant flurry.

EARTH AND I GAVE YOU TURQUOISE[1]

Earth and I gave you turquoise
      when you walked singing
We lived laughing in my house
      and told old stories
You grew ill when the owl cried
We will meet on Black Mountain

I will bring corn for planting
      and we will make fire
Children will come to your breast
      You will heal my heart
I speak your name many times
The wild cane remembers you

My young brother's house is filled
      I go there to sing
We have not spoken of you
      But our songs are sad
When Moon Woman goes to you
I will follow her white way

Tonight they dance near Chinle
      by the seven elms
There your loom whispered beauty
      They will eat mutton
and drink coffee till morning
You and I will not be there

I saw a crow by Red Rock
      standing on one leg
It was the black of your hair
      The years are heavy
I will ride the swiftest horse
You will hear the drumming hooves

[1] Turquoise has long occupied a prominent place in the mythology and folklore of the Indians of the Southwest. Indian tradition attributes many virtues to it, such as possessing the mystic power to help, protect and bring good fortune to the wearer.

PIT VIPER

The cordate head[1] meanders through himself:
Metamorphosis. Slowly the new thing,
Kindled to flares along his length, curves out.
From the evergreen shade where he has lain,
Through inland seas and catacombs he moves.
Blurred eyes that ever see have seen him waste,
Acquire, and undiminished: have seen death—
Or simile—come nigh and overcome.
Alone among his kind, old, almost wise,
Mere hunger cannot urge him from this drowse.

[1] Heart shaped

BUTEO REGALIS[2]

His frailty discrete, the rodent turns, looks.
What sense first warns? The winging is unheard,
Unseen but as distant motion made whole,
Singular, slow, unbroken in its glide.
It veers, and veering, tilts broad-surfaced wings.
Aligned, the span bends to begin the dive
And falls, alternately white and russet,
Angle and curve, gathering momentum.

[2] Buteo refers to any of a genus of large, broad-winged, soaring hawks that prey on rodents. The Buteo Regalis is one of two species of the rough-legged hawk.

Duane Niatum

A TRIBUTE TO CHIEF JOSEPH (1840?–1904)

Never reaching the promised land in Canada,
HIN-MAH-TOO-YAH-LAT-KET: "Thunder-rolling-in-the-mountains,"
the fugitive chief sits in a corner
of the prison car headed for Oklahoma,
chained to his warriors,
a featherless hawk in exile.

He sees out the window
geese rise from the storm's center
and knows more men died
by snow blizzard
than by cavalry shot.

Still his father's shield
of Wallowa Valley deer and elk
flashes in his eyes
as coyote runs the circles
and a cricket swallows the dark.

How many songs this elder
sang to break the cycle
of cold weather and disease
his people coughed and breathed
in this land of drifting ice.

Now sleepless as the door-guard,
the train rattles like dirt in his teeth,
straw in his eyes.
Holding rage in the palm of his fist,
his people's future spirals to red-forest dust.

leaves his bones on the track,
his soul in the whistle.

THE WATERFALL SONG
(for Rona)

From their first dawn, he embraced the night sensations;
she who danced with him into the burning words.
He wanted to feel her turn as the river turns,
she who danced with him into the burning words.

He stepped toward the song she offered in the dark;
she whose voice could stir the sparrow's heart.
He asked for her hand because his life was there.
She whose voice could stir the sparrow's heart.

He landscaped her home with the rarest stone;
she planted the seeds that brought the wild to bloom.
He carved her a bird the water filled with spirit.
She planted the seeds that brought the wild to bloom.

He saw from her eyes the waterfall was blue;
and it was she that changed the seasons of the wind.
And in their solitude he gave nakedness the field,
since it was she who kept the colors in the fall.

THE OWL IN THE REARVIEW MIRROR

It was a miracle he glimpsed an owl sway
sideways through his eye. He watched it roll
back from the hills, hills ebbing like glaciers;
swing across the sky like a pendulum.
Does it follow stars through wheat fields
because hunger calls, or moon is luminous?
Does it tell him, not to ram the oak?
As is, the bird seems content to shift his roots,
plant him like a sapling in snow. For it
pulls him into the back seat and out the window
by the power of its agile, silent wing.
He is the mouse paralyzed by its shadow dance.
So he goes further, lets it drive him home,
leave his soul soaring for the yellow sky.

SONG FROM THE TOTEM MAKER

Why not view your family's past
from a less weathered shore?
You have a chance to forgive your wounds.
For you were the boy who often wished
he had burned his ancestors' longhouse
to the ground. Besides, you could never
blame the village shaker;
it was his stories that brought you comfort.

They showed how to see the owl
settle in the four directions, hear
the river run for salmon's way.
They cleared the path to where First People
circled until your feelings had wings,
to ease the morning's weight on your eyelids,
bury your pride in confusion's cave.

And I offered you when young a light
burden, seven days of rain, and another storm.
You saw the water dreamers run away with hope:
Thunderbird because he's entombed in clay,
teeth, and shell; Raven because it can't see
the sun touch the crocus beneath the ferns
without laughing so hard it thunders.

The water dreamers also ran away
because bluejay watched the people miss his
humor, his praise to the women who swam
the river; whale because it's now desert dust.
Beaver because his last dam demolished
the rainbow that held up the stars.
Since beaver didn't keep his nose to the current.

the winter floods took his dam to another country.
And you never appreciated the time wolf
roamed through your terror of the forest's
destruction. But he'll stop when you stop
running from the dead and the cave drummers.
So the next dawn wolf calls to you,
listen to his rattle that shakes you to shore,

as it was your ignorance that started the tremor
that led the sharks to your dying village,
the dwindling stream inching toward the breakers.

Calvin O'John

DANCING TEEPEES

Dancing teepees
High up in the Rocky Mountains,
Dancing teepees
Dance on the grassy banks of Cripple Creek
With laughing fringes in the autumn sun.
Indian children
Play with bows and arrows
On the grassy banks of Cripple Creek.
Indian women
Gather kindling
To start an evening fire,
Dancing teepees
Dance against fire-lighted autumn trees.
Braves returning
Home from raiding,
Gallantly ride into camp
With horses, scalps, and ornaments.
Dancing teepees,
Sleep now on the grassy banks of Cripple Creek
High up in the Rocky Mountains.

Simon Ortiz

TEN O'CLOCK NEWS

berstein disc jockey
telling about indians
on ten o'clock news
o they have been screwed
i know everybody's talking
about indians yesterday
murdering conquest the buffalo
in those hills in kansas
railroad hustling progress
today maybe tomorrow in
ghost dance dreams we'll
find out berstein doesn't know
what indians say these days
in wino translations
he doesn't know that and even
indians sometimes don't know
because they believe in trains
and what berstein tells them
on ten o'clock news

THIS PREPARATION

these sticks i am holding
i cut down at the creek.
i have just come from there.
i listened to the creek
speaking to the world,
i did my praying,
and then i took my knife
and cut the sticks.
there is some sorrow in leaving
fresh wounds in growing things,
but my praying has relieved
some of my sorrow. prayers
make things possible, my uncle said.
before i left i listened again
for words the creek was telling,
and i smelled its smell which
are words also. and then
i tied my sticks into a bundle
and came home, each step a prayer
for this morning and a safe return.
my son is sleeping still
in this quietness, my wife
is stirring at her cooking,
and i am making this preparation.
i wish to make my praying
into these sticks like gods have taught.

SMOKING MY PRAYERS

now that i have lighted my smoke
i am motioning to the east
i am walking in thought that direction
i am listening for your voices
i am occurring in my mind
            this instance that i am here
now that i have breathed inwards
i am seeing the mountains east
i am travelling to that place of birth
i am aware of your voices
i am thinking of your relationship with me
            this time in the morning that we are together
now that i have breathed outwards
i am letting you take my breath
i am moving for your sake
i am hearing the voices of your children
i am not myself but yourself now
            at this time your spirit has captured mine
now that i am taking breath in again
i have arrived back from that place of birth
i have travelled fast and surely
i have heard what you wanted me to hear
i have become whole and strong with yourself

            this morning i am living with your breath.

RELOCATION

don't talk to me no words
don't frighten me
for i am in the blinding city
the lights
the cars
the deadened glares
      tear my heart
      and close my mind
who questions my pain
the tight knot of anger
in my breast
i swallow hard and often
and taste my spit
and it does not taste good
who questions my mind

i came here because i was tired
the BIA taught me to cleanse myself
daily to keep a careful account of my time
efficiency was learned in catechism
the sisters spelled me good in white
and i came here to feed myself
corn and potatoes and chili and mutton
did not nourish me it was said
so i agreed to move
i seem walking in sleep
down streets down streets grey with cement
and glaring glass and oily wind
armed with a pint of wine

i cheated the children to buy
i am ashamed
i am tired
i am hungry
i speak words
i am lonely for hills
i am lonely for myself

Agnes Pratt

DEATH TAKES ONLY A MINUTE

Agonies of change
can be heard
in the lonely silence
of a single raindrop
bending a leaf downward.

All this is distant
and will fade further back
when my relatives assemble to haggle
over the price of dying.

EMPATHY

Our glances spin silver threads,
Weaving a web of closeness;
Catching, holding
A love too tenuous for words.
Woven and remembered
In silence, those hours
When time had something
To do with the moon.

Stay, or flee
As you must—
Uncountable the ways
We seek ourselves
I will keep
The interwoven strands of you
As I keep the enduring moon
And its web of shadow.

Fred Red Cloud

A TALE OF LAST STANDS

His hair was yellow and long
    and shone like singing hills
    There were times when he
    spoke as our friend
    and waved the branch of peace.

But the night in the Metropolitan Hotel
    when he wrote the unremembered
    truth that his ambition
    trampled old words into dust,
    the night he threw splinters
    of justice onto the floor and
    promised death to Sitting Bull,

That night he lost his name
    of honor with my people.
    What was to be his ambush
    of us, turned out to be
    our ambush of him.

Now the tumbleweeds blow down
    cemetery rows of Indian
    and trooper. Little streams
    wander restlessly in the
    low hills and yesterdays
    blur into sluggish tomorrows.

Rain and wind and sun
    float leisurely over the
    land of the Little Big Horn
    and the wild duck's cry
    drifts down from eternal heights.

My people felt the shock of
    national defeat in battles
    that followed. Our war shirts
    were hung on prison walls,
    and reservations fused us into
    a sleep-muddied people.

The heel of time walked on
    and now the white man
    watches the mountain waters
    crash against his empire.

I sit with eyes like brown wounds
    and remember a yellow-haired laugh
    in a place where
    tumbleweeds blow
    and I think of Dien Bien Phu,
    and Belgian Congo, other Aryan
    last stands, sacrificial totem games,
    and a bitter laugh
sprawls across my memory-wrinkled face.

Now . . . others ride the black-bones
    horse of sorrow
    as I watch from the shadows of time.

MACHU PICCHU, PERU[1]

A railroad suddenly hops out of the
        quartz mountain. Edges of time
        explode at the eyes, painful as
        a child's nightmare. Double-jointed
        rivers stretch toward purple,
        cantilevered mountains honed
        by the leather sky as the steam
        engine coughs like a widow in
        church. 12,000 feet. Cuzqueno
        Indian babies sit straight as
        daisies. An airplane stutters
        overhead. A net of sky falls
        on the hardness of speed here,
        near the fabled Bridge of
        San Luis Rey.

Below . . . a stone shelf holding an
        offering, a small inn, fragile as
        first frost. The sky becomes a
        beggar, leans forward and holds out
        an alms bowl. My ears crack with
        the sharpness of a spine of clay
        in a Lima potter's hand. Height
        soaks away. We are where lizards
        play in the ruined stone of
        Machu Picchu. Smells of history.
        are copper at the nose, here,
        where Angels fall. My feet touch
        the 3000-stone path of Inca princes
        and fairy tales dribble from the
        mouths of the betel-stained guides.

[1] An ancient fortress city in the Peruvian Andes, about 50 miles northeast of
Cuzco.

Carter Revard

THE COYOTE

There was a little rill of water, near the den,
That showed a trickle, all the dry summer
When I was born. One night in late August it rained;
The thunder waked us. Drops came crashing down
In dust, on stiff blackjack leaves, on lichened rocks,
Rain came in a pelting rush down over the hill,
Wind puffed wet into the cave; I heard sounds
Of leaf-drip, rustle of soggy branches in gusts of wind.

And then the rill's tune changed: I heard a rock drop
And set new ripples gurgling in a lower key.
Where the new ripples were, I drank, next morning,
Fresh muddy water that set my teeth on edge.
I thought how delicate that rock's poise was:
The storm made music, when it changed my world.

ON THE BRIGHT SIDE

When the green grass rose in the spring
        our Jersey's milk turned yellow
    with cream and tasted musky
        with different weed-flavors; and she'd
    be bellowing to be milked
before the sun got up—which was all right,
        it gave us longer days, especially weekends.
One disadvantage though
        of getting up so early

was that we'd generally watch the sun come up,
        and mornings when it was red and slow
we'd make a game of staring at its rising
    until our eyes were filled with slow
                    blood-bubbles and
            gold balloons floating
transparently over meadows with
    birds winging darkly through them—
this blinded us of course
            to other things,
        so when we went to breakfast
inside the flyspecked house the air was dim
        as a cathedral, with white glasses
            of milk standing calmly
                for hands to reach and bring
    their creamy coldness up
to dazzled eyes and mouth,
        and the chunk of butter melting
        into the bowl of hot oatmeal
            swam out of focus like
    a tiny sun as we poured
flurries of sugar-crystals down from spoons upon it
            and stirred in Jersey cream, then
                    crumbled the toast-with-butter in it
and spooned up crunch-chewy pieces
                    like morning sunlight
    while the roaches went scrambling for crumbs
    on threadbare oilcloth and our fledgling
                wild goldfinch chirruped, waiting
for the fattened roaches we'd bring him on pins as soon
            as the sun got out of our eyes
                and into our hungry bellies.

Ronald Rogers

TAKING OFF

1
Barely did the dust settle
huddle down
than the wind blew
kicked it up
slapped me right in the eyes.

"Oh, Hell," I said.

2
The dust sits on everything
everyone
on the streets
on everyone
I blow (whew)
to clean them off.

They cloud up.

3
I stuff my bag
full of clothes
the road is dusty
the road sign is dusty
my thumb is dusty
I blink.

Somebody gives me a ride.

4
The car starts up
we're off
the road is smooth
zump zump zump
go the white paint lines
beneath us.

I feel superior.

5
The driver asks me
"Where are you going?"
"Beg pardon?" I say
The driver laughs
slaps my back
the dust blooms up
I cough.

I tell him to stop the car.

6
I am sitting on my bag
I sigh
I put out my thumb
zzem
goes a car.
The dust swirls up.

KINDERGARTEN

In my kindergarten class
there were windows around the room
and in the morning we all took naps.
We brought our own rugs and crayons
because that was responsibility
and we learned to tell the colors apart.

Sometimes we read stories
about wrinkled old pirates with parrots
who talked about cities of gold.
And then we'd talk about cities of gold
with streets of silver
and we'd laugh and laugh and laugh.

The floors were all made of wood
in long, long strips—
brown wood with un-peely wax.
One day the toughest kid in school
got mad and yelled at the teacher
and we smiled when he went to the principal.

The principal had a long black whip
studded through with razor blades
and nine lashes on it.
The principal wore a black suit
and smoked Pall Malls
and wrote bad notes to your father.

In my kindergarten class
there were windows around the room
and in the morning we all took naps.
We brought our own rugs and crayons
because that was responsibility
and we learned to tell the colors apart.

Wendy Rose

CAGED WINGS: FIRST IMPRESSIONS FROM THE BOAT ALCATRAZ ISLAND/INDIAN LAND, 1970

Broken plaster wings,
loose feathers in a dance
together, bend encaged
the vision
of western eyes tight
and cold into walls
that stink of humanity
pulstate forbidden
life; in the plaster
charred places, pomegranate paint
dripped to the floor
from graffiti and ice
thin enough to skip
on the edge of the fog.
We must not be walking here
heavy-footed, merely human,
for we need to fly
this one time and
be drumming our wings
close together, clouding our eyes
with ourselves and
not be led away.

The rain comes little
by little each day
and the mist
thins and billows
beneath the steel bridge.
There is a song at our center
and a campfire crackling
with the rags and branches that built it
to keep out the Coast Guard, make bright
the night that would hide
helicopters and guns. At midnight
the singers shine
and beat the drum of
a new kind of sun.

Wendy Rose

I EXPECTED MY SKIN AND MY BLOOD TO RIPEN

"When the blizzard subsided four days later (after the massacre), a burial party was sent to Wounded Knee. A long trench was dug. Many of the bodies were stripped by whites who went out in order to get the ghost shirts and other accoutrements the Indians wore . . . the frozen bodies were thrown into the trench stiff and naked . . . only a handful of items remain in private hands . . . exposure to snow has stiffened the leggings and moccasins, and all the objects show the effects of age and long use. . . . " There follows: Moccasins at $140, hide scraper at $350, buckskin shirt at $1200, woman's leggings at $275, bone breastplate at $1000.
        Plains Indian Art: Sales Catalog by Kenneth Canfield, 1977

I expected my skin and my blood
to ripen
not be ripped from my bones;
like green fruit I am peeled
tasted, discarded; my seeds are stepped on
and crushed
as if there were no future. Now
there has been
no past.   My own body gave up the beads
my own arms handed the babies away
to be strung on bayonets, to be counted
one by one like rosary stones and then
to be tossed to each side of life
as if the pain of their borning
had never been.

My feet were frozen to the leather,
pried apart, left behind—bits of flesh
on the moccasins, bits of papery deerhide
on the bones. My back was stripped
of its cover, its quilling intact; was torn,
was taken away, was restored.
My leggings were taken like in a rape
and shriveled to the size of stick figures
like they had never felt
the push of my strong woman's body
walking in the hills.
It was my own baby whose cradleboard I held.
Would've put her in my mouth
like a snake
if I could, would've turned her
into a bush or old rock
if there'd been enough magic
to work such changes. Not enough magic
even to stop the bullets.
Not enough magic
to stop the scientists.
Not enough magic
to stop the collectors.

Norman H. Russell

THE EYES OF THE CHILD DO NOT SEE ME

i look into the eyes of the child
the eyes of the child do not see me
the eyes of the child look somewhere else

i look down at the sand
the child has a stick in his hand
the child makes pictures in the sand

what do the pictures mean?
what do the eyes of the child see?

i speak to the child
i ask him what he draws in the sand
the child looks at me and says nothing

the child arises and runs into the forest
i sit still looking a long time at his pictures
something in the sand is speaking to me.

THE WORLD HAS MANY PLACES MANY WAYS

in the forest hearing
the anger of the black and yellow
wasp in the old tree going
down the sky to the eating
mouth of the earth i walk
a new path around i cannot
speak friend words to
this creature who
only speaks war

in the black night coming
out of the black lake water
mists of mosquitoes seeking
blood of my body i cover
myself with the blanket waiting
the sun of the morning which sends
the night creatures flying
into the trees and the waters
their secret homes to hide

one goes his way with wise feet
one walks with open eyes
one sleeps in his own places
the man has his place in the world
the world has many places many ways
only the creature who leaves his own place
only the creature who walks another's way
will be killed will be eaten.

THE GREAT WAY OF THE MAN

the eagle's eye is the strongest eye
the arm of the bear is the strongest arm
nothing flies so well as the swallow
nothing swims so fast as the fish
nothing runs so quick as the deer
nor leaps so far as the panther
the wolverine's teeth are the strongest teeth
the yellow wasp has the greatest poison
every animal has its one thing
every animal has its one great way

which is the great way of the man?
what is the thing that he does?

the man goes everywhere and does everything
the man sees almost as well as the eagle
the man runs almost as fast as the deer
the man swims almost as fast as the fish

the man is more cunning than the fox
the man is more cunning than all the animals
the gods of the man are more powerful
than the gods of the animals.

CLERK'S SONG II

what does the forest do monday through friday?
i was a boy; i knew; now i have forgotten
all my dreams are dying
all my dreams are dead

i leave at night i return at night
what does the world do during the day
the world works the world works
all my dreams are dying

young girls lie on beaches young boys play
this is what the world does during the day
i read my newspaper
all my dreams are dying

i am going to a white hell there will be
typewriters typing file cases standing
secretaries with spread legs
all my dreams are dying

when i turn the television off silence comes
like a black cloak and holds me
trembling trembling
all my dreams are dead.

Bruce Severy

POEMS

my poems
are the sounds
of pigeons
feathering the moonlight.

feathering the twitch
in the eye
of a hawk
heavy with hoot sleep.

DESERTED FARMS POEM

alone hunting.
on the hill behind
a deserted farm gone awry.
junk strewn about.
wrecked by vandals.
by Tyrkir, a mercenary, a German.
by Thorhall, later lost.
by Eirik the Red.
found Vinland: old way of saying.
astragalus.
oxytropis, maydelliana.
vetch.
locoweed.
a cow's jaw on the prairie.
teeth of the old ships
scattered around.

OPENING DAY

I hear ghosts of grouse
in wheat stubble
or late barley.

grouse ghosts
eat buffalo berries
and cluck.

but they never fly out.

I walk all day.

I hunt.

I hear shots banging out of empty guns.

until the sun
goes back to the lake.

I have many birds
inside me
                already.

STRUGGLE FOR THE ROADS

prairie grass:

new sprouts
in the tire ruts
of the dirt roads.

trucks and buses
roll out the roads
like dough:

trucks and buses
and the seasons
of new dust.

but night creatures
keep reseeding
from invisible bags of seeds.

and sky gods water
from secret ponds
hidden in the stars
of the upper limbs
of the cottonwoods.

FIRST AND LAST

as the first congress
was called:
assembly of elders,
assembly of soldiers:

as the first issue of debate
was debated
against Kish, first given
after the flood:

as the first vote
was taken:
Gilgamesh voted there:

as the first sanction of war
was passed down:
and: as the war
was lost:
as all wars have been lost:

as I, chronicler,
inscribe this
in the lasting clay
of the banked Tigris:

the river that flows
first and last:
through the uneven land
of our memory.

Loyal Shegonee

LONELINESS

The deafening tic-tic-tic of the clock,
The thunder of my own thoughts rumble 'round
The dark room crowding its silence in upon me.
Where are my friends? What is there to do?
The slow steady pounding of my lonesome heart,
The never-ending thump-thump-thump of my pulse
Against a wet pillow, the only living sounds to listen to!
Visions drift slowly past my eyes . . .
Visions of scarred, contorted trees standing in barren,
                                    desolate fields . . .
Visions of solitary children standing in deserted alleys
With tears washing clean rivulets down their dirty faces . . .
Visions of old men, old women, dying with hopelessness
And agony twisted into their aged masks of death . . .
Visions of neglected tombstones crumbling by
Abandoned churches . . . Oh God!
Where are my friends?
Someone, please come and talk to me!

Soge Track

INDIAN LOVE LETTER

Lady of the crescent moon
tonight I look at the sky
You are not there
You are not mad at me, are you?
"You are angry at the people,
Yes, I know."
           they are changing
           be not too hard
If you were taken to
the mission school,
not because you wanted,
but someone thought it best for you
you too would change.

They came out of nowhere
telling us how to eat our food
how to build our homes
how to plant our crops.
Need I say more of what they did?
All is new—the old ways are nothing.
           they are changing
           be not too hard
I talk to them
they turn their heads.
Do not be hurt—you have me
I live by the old ways
I will not change.

Tonight—my prayer plumes in hand
with the white shell things—
to the silent place I will go
(It is for you I go, please be there.)
Oh! Lady of the crescent moon
with the corn-silk hair—I love you[1]
    they are changing
    be not too hard

[1] According to Navajo mythology, Hasjelti and Hostjoghon were the children of Ahsonnutli, the turquoise, and Yolaikaiason (white-shell woman, wife of the Sun). Ahsonnutli placed an ear of white corn and Yolaikaiason an ear of yellow corn on the mountain where the fogs meet. The corn conceived, the white corn giving birth to Hasjelti and the yellow corn to Hostjoghon. These two became the great song-makers of the world. They gave to the mountain of their nativity (Henry Mountain in Utah) two songs and two prayers; they then went to Sierra Blanca (Colorado) and made two songs and prayers and dressed the mountain in clothing of white shell with two eagle plumes placed upright upon the head.

Also, according to myth, when the Indians see the silk on the cornstalk they are reminded of the beautiful woman with long light hair who has not forgotten them.

Winifred Fields Walters

NAVAJO SIGNS

How can you know, or understand, our loss
The rough-edged feel of poverty that came
to us in broken treaties' scourging hour?
Your skin is much too pale, or else too black
(Though white or colored skin is not the point).
You never lived with legend, ancient tales,
Told many times around a hogan fire
While bitter winter sapped the very flames.
You never slept an infant's passive sleep
Bound in a cradleboard, handcarved and laced
The way the Holy Ones taught us in days
Long past, beyond our farthest memory.
You never tended sheep in lambing time
Nor watched lambs frolic, stiff-kneed, in the rain.
You never knew serenity of life
In tune with nature's balanced give and take,
That total, grateful sense of solitude,
That prayer of thanks breathed out for hunter's skill,
A prayer which reaches silently to the
Great Source, as close in red rock canyons as
In rich and hallowed chapels made by men.
To you, tradition seems a binding thing,
But there are those of us who turn ourselves,
At least within our hearts, to that which was,
And was so handsomely; reluctant still
To lay away such beauty and such peace,
As brotherhood beyond the clan or tribe,
That precious dignity in which a people walked
The pollen path: that timeless way,
So simple, so complex, so nearly gone.

Archie Washburn

HOGAN

Hogan
Sitting against
The flying dust of wind.
Here and there flows the old raggy
Long johns.

UNKNOWN SMOKE

Out in the far distance away
I saw a cloud of smoke
Flowing into the gentle air,
Wondering what it was from here
Where I was standing all puzzled up,
With a sway of clean fresh air
Blowing through my black crisp hair.

Not knowing what it really was I stood
With strong sorrow break-down,
With many known and unknown voices
In the background of my image.
Looking around with astonishment it looked on my
Face among the crowds with many unknown
And known faces of the crowd.

Wishing what was happpening
In the far distance in the west,
Everything turned out clear with a siren
Sounding through the town going towards west.
The siren sounded loud and turned out with faded sound
In the distant far away.
Still the smoke floated around in the clear day.
Wondering what was happening in the distance,
I only know that it's an unknown smoke in
The far distance in the west.

James Welch

HARLEM, MONTANA: JUST OFF THE RESERVATION

We need no runners here. Booze is law
and all the Indians drink in the best tavern.
Money is free if you're poor enough.
Disgusted, busted whites are running
for office in this town wise enough
to qualify for laughter. The constable,
a local farmer, plants and the jail with wild
raven-haired stiffs who beg just one more drink.
One drunk, a former Methodist, becomes a saint
in the Indian church, bugs the plaster man
on the cross with snakes. If his knuckles broke,
he'd see those women wail the graves goodbye.

Goodbye, goodbye, Harlem on the rocks,
so bigoted, you forget the latest joke,
so lonely, you'd welcome a battalion of Turks
to rule your women. What you don't know,
what you will never know or want to learn—
Turks aren't white. Turks are olive, unwelcome,
alive in any town. Turks would use
your one dingy park to declare a need for loot.
Turks say bring it, step quickly, lay down and dead.

Here we are when men were nice. This photo, hung
in the New England Hotel lobby, show them nicer
than pie, agreeable to the warring bands of redskins
who demanded protection money for the price of food.
Now, only Hutterites out north are nice. We hate
them. They are tough and their crops are always good.
We accuse them of idiocy and believe their belief all wrong.

Harlem, your hotel is overnamed, your children
are raggedy-assed but you go on, survive
the bad food from the two cafes that peddle
your hate for the wild who bring you money.
When you die, if you die, will you remember
The three young bucks who shot the grocery up,
locked themselves in and cried for days, we're rich,
help us, oh God, we're rich.

THE MAN FROM WASHINGTON

The end came easy for most of us.
Packed away in our crude beginnings
in some far corner of a flat world,
we didn't expect much more
than firewood and buffalo robes
to keep us warm. The man came down,
a slouching dwarf with rainwater eyes,
and spoke to us. He promised
that life would go on as usual,
that treaties would be signed, and everyone—
man, woman and child—would be innoculated
against a world in which we had no part,
a world of wealth, promise and fabulous disease.

DREAMING WINTER

Don't ask me if these knives are real.
I could paint a king or show a map
the way home—to go like this:
wobble me back to a tiger's dream,
a dream of knives and bones too common
to be exposed. My secrets are ignored.

Here comes the man I love. His coat is wet
and his face is falling like the leaves,
tobacco stains on his Polish teeth.
I could tell jokes about him—one up
for the man who brags a lot, laughs
a little and hangs his name on the nearest knob.
Don't ask me. I know it's only hunger.

I saw that king—the one my sister knew
but was allergic to. Her face ran until
his eyes became the white of several winters.
Snow on his bed told him that the silky tears
were uniformly mad and all the money in the world
couldn't bring him to a tragic end. Shame
or fortune tricked me to his table, shattered
my one standing lie with new kinds of fame.

Have mercy on me. Lord, really. If I should die
before I wake, take me to that place I just heard
banging in my ears. Don't ask me. Let me join
the other kings, the ones who trade their knives
for a sack of keys. Let me open any door,
stand winter still and drown in a common dream.

ONE MORE TIME

1.

Where he really hung, there
on the tree, a promising star
and great child of wonder,
I sit in memory of yellow lights,
the fantasies of lovely aunts
at Christmas time. The Eve
astounds itself with a pale snow.

Children in their socks rush by me,
bent on odd deliveries—the promise
a child made them years ago
before we felt the twinge
of common guilt. How far
we have come, how sacred is the snow
that eats like cancer at our bones.

2.

How many women say, Child, wrap me
in your camel robe, lay me down,
spread in the straw and chaff
of all my poor loves' salvation.
Tender me, Child, one quick kiss
before your terrible road strikes off
the broad fantasies of your mother's way.

3.

I am basking in the white rain
of my father's seed. I do not wish
to come, to coat the limbs of my
father's tree a second time.
The salvation's in my bones like cancer
and I wish to die like men.

Roberta Hill Whiteman

STAR QUILT

These are notes to lightning in my bedroom.
A star forged from linen thread and patches.
Purple, yellow, red like diamond suckers, children

of the star gleam on sweaty nights. The quilt unfolds
against sheets, moving, warm clouds of Chinook.
It covers my cuts, my red birch clusters under pine.

Under it your mouth begins a legend,
and wide as the plain, I hope Wisconsin marshes
promise your caress. The candle locks

us in forest smells, your cheek tattered
by shadow. Sweetened by wings, my mothlike heart
flies nightly among geraniums.

We know of land that looks lonely,
but isn't, of beef with hides of velveteen,
of sorrow, an eddy in blood.

Star quilt, sewn from dawn light by fingers
of flint, take away those touches
meant for noisier skins,

anoint us with grass and twilight air,
so we may embrace, two bitter roots
pushing back into the dust.

OVERCAST DAWN

This morning I feel dreams dying.
One trace is this feather
fallen from a gull,
with its broken shaft,
slight white down,
and long dark tip
that won't hold air.
How will you reach me
if all our dreams are dead?
Will I find myself
as empty as an image,
that death mask of a woman
reflected in car windows?
Help me, for every bird
remembers as it preens
the dream that lifted
it to flight.
Help me, for the sky
is close with feathers,
falling today
from sullen clouds.

VARIATIONS FOR TWO VOICES

I

Where do we live?
  Underneath sunset.
How long have we been here?
  Since your grandfather's death
  when war came without effort
  and hearts didn't own
  a tear or a victory.
  We stand in a stranger's field
  beyond pardon.
What do we do?
  We hide. We bargain.
  We answer each question
  with a difficult anger,
  map the future for heartache
  and rattle old bones.
When is it time?
  Time is that beggar
  living in the basement.
  He dictates to us
  when to move, how to dream.
  Run and he'll be there
  waiting at crossroads,
  with pitch for your ribcage
  and pins for your eyes.
Who'll come to save us?
  No one, Nothing.
  Yet when the wind stirs
  I hear voices call us
  inside the snow drift.
  I've heard it those nights
  when snow writhes before Spring.
  Don't ever listen.
  Don't ever listen.
  Don't listen. What
  it can bring!

II

Where do we live?
  Inside this morning.
How long have we been here?
  Only the lakes remember
  our arrival. Go there at dawn
  when reeds ride the slow wash.
  An answer will come
  from the small world of crayfish.
What do we do?
  Balance our shadows
  like oaks in bright sunlight,
  stretch and tumble
  as much as we're able,
  eat up the light
  and struggle with blindness.
When is it time?
  Time is a thrush
  that preens in the wood
  and sings on a slender branch
  in your ribcage. Listen
  to what comes on invisible wings
  darting above the blue roots
  of flowers. Fly, Dragon
  fly. Now the bird sings.
Who'll come to save us?
  For some, it's the rattling
  cloud, the air before evening.
  Come, take my hand,
  for all that it's worth.
  Our hearts learn
  much too soon
  how to speak like mountain
  stones.

Donna Whitewing

AUGUST 24, 1963—1:00 A.M.—OMAHA

Heavy breathing fills all my chamber
Sinister trucks prowl
        down dim-lit alleyways.
Racing past each other,
            cars toot obscenities.
Silence is crawling in open windows
            smiling and warm.
Suddenly,
            crickets and cockroaches
            join in the madness:
            cricking and crawling
Here I am!
A portion of some murky design.
Writing,
        because I cannot sleep,
        because I could die here.

A VEGETABLE, I WILL NOT BE

Who would suspect, or even know
    the ivory-white innocence
    of steaming hot cake:

Not you?
Let me tell you something.
Wheat grows a pure gold coat.
Grazing is plush green plunder.
Well,
    it ought to be splendid!
Wheat, fed on bones
    for its white flesh,
    ate gold teeth from skulls
    scattered through the yard,
        for a coat.
Green grasses:
    from green flesh at full moon.
Harvesting wheat,
    a man fell dead from heart attacks.
To the Sod!
This hot cake is moist
    and steams of three tablespoons milk—
    from a dying cow.
When time stretches me to nothing,
    read instructions of my burial carefully.
It's all taped to the bottom
    of an oatmeal box—
    third cupboard to the left as you enter the kitchen,
    bottom shelf.
It reads:

    "Lay me low in the wheat yards.
    Fill my head with gold teeth.
    I could not risk grassing to cows for milk;
    Cows dry up sometimes.
    I'd rather be a hot cake.
    I will not be a bowl.
            of peas!"

Ray Young Bear

WRONG KIND OF LOVE

he placed the medicine
over the skillet
which held glowing ashes.
then with a blanket
he formed himself
into a small hill.
it grew each time
he inhaled. a song
followed making everything
complete: the girl who
possessed him would soon
realize the powers of
the northern medicine men.

WARRIOR DREAMS

he said, i want to be wrapped
inside the american flag.
there will be small kettles
of food my mother prepared
around my body.   i will be
so proud you will feel as
if it was really intended.
my brothers are flag toles
and soon songs will flow
me into them.   no one is going
to cry because they never
really knew me.   when the old
men lower me into the earth
one tear will appear on
a side of my eye.   it will
roll a little ways and then stop.

EMPTY STREAMS OF AUTUMN

A bible opens then closes real hard
down the dirt road. The wind from the slam
tells a story of a preacher who mumbles far
away from the Church because he has read
the good words to his children
and he listened.

Indians at the gathering sing songs
so that young boys are protected from
death on lands across the oceans.
Six who died stand and whisper
these words songs never crossed the oceans. . . .

The red fox hears this and turns running
with his front feet over his eyes
so the sun does not blind him.
In the morning he will drown
under the icy waters of the river
that was not there four days ago.

They said a naked brown baby
without arms crawled from under
the flag and shouted obscenities
to the cloudless grey sky.

The thin bird flew high above
the reaching old tree starving for wind.
A small boy began to chop the tree
because the shack needed firewood
so his mother would die in warmth.

The fences shivered throughout the night
and on the wire were hawks that
flew after the sun.
In the morning
the thin bird cried when he
found corn under the wet snow. . . .

ONE CHIP OF HUMAN BONE

One chip of human bone.

it is almost fitting
to die on the railroad tracks.
i can easily understand
how they felt on their
staggered walks back.

there is something about
trains, drinking, and being
an indian with nothing to lose.

THE LISTENING ROCK

the blueness of night
grows quietly whispering
at each thought
you have heard of the rock
which lies over fog.
we are almost so magic
and i breathe wings
that brush the smoke
disappearing inside bodies.
below the river is day
clear and rushing faster.
it swallows the meaning
of moon and people
quiet within the pines
killing four sleeping robins.
a body wrapped in a flag
was never seen as glory
until our father asked us
to help even when we were
dying. he knew of these
colors and never asked for
reasons. earth heard them
talking to themselves
far away and always spoke
back: you are home.
the morning came while she
peeled the potatoes for
breakfast and it was then
i felt as a part blending
beautifully but not knowing
where to go.   the rock ate
before us it was given
words by her reminding
our grandfathers to
search for us when the
rain falls and we do not hear.

Biographical Sketches

Paula Allen, a Sioux-Laguna, was born in Cubero, New Mexico, in 1939. After receiving an M.F.A. from Oregon and a Ph.D. from the University of New Mexico, she went on to teach at Fort Lewis College in Durango, Colorado, then became Chairman of Native American Studies at San Francisco State. "Lament of My Father, Lakota" previously appeared in *The South Dakota Review*, 1973.

Carroll Arnett/Gogisgi was born in Oklahoma City in 1927 of Cherokee-French ancestry. After serving in the Marine Corps, he went on to study at the University of Oklahoma, Beloit College, and the University of Texas. He is currently Professor of English at Central Michigan University. He is the author of several volumes of poetry. "Out in the Woods" and "The Story of My Life" appeared in *Tsalagi* (The Elizabeth Press, 1976).

Liz Sohappy Bahe was given in 1969 her Palouse name, Om-na-ma, which was that of her great-grandmother on her father's side. She says of this: "My Indian name has made a great difference in my life. I really felt like a floating body until I received my name. My grandmother said that is how it was to be—no one is here on earth until he has an Indian name." Liz attended the Institute of American Indian Arts for most of two years and then studied art in Portland, Oregon, for a time. "Once Again" appeared previously in *The South Dakota Review*.

Charles G. Ballard is a Quapaw-Cherokee scholar. He taught English at the Chilocco Indian School for seven years and for three years at Northern Oklahoma College, Tonkawa. He is now at Idaho State University. He received his B.A. and M.A. from Oklahoma State University at Stillwater.

Jim Barnes was born in Oklahoma in 1931 of Choctaw descent. He received his B.A. at Southeastern State College in Oklahoma, before going on to complete his M.A. and Ph.D. at the University of Arkansas. He currently teaches at Northeast Missouri State University. "Contemporary Native American Poetry" originally appeared in the *Mississippi Valley Review*; "The Chicago Odyssey" appeared in *Shantih*; and "Autobiographical Flashback: Puma and Pokeweed" appeared in the *Long Pond Review*. All three poems were reprinted in his *The American Book of the Dead* (U. of Illinois Press, 1982).

Peter Blue Cloud/Aroniawenrate, a member of the Turtle clan, Mohawk Nation, was born at Caughnawaga Reserve in Quebec in 1927. A poet, carpenter and wood carver, he is also a former editor of *Akwesasne Notes*. "Sweetgrass" previously appeared in *White Corn Sister* (Strawberry Press, 1977).

Joseph Bruchac, Abenaki on his mother's side, was born in Saratoga Springs, New York, in 1942. He received a B.A. from Cornell University and an M.A. from Syracuse University. Widely published in anthologies and journals and author of several volumes of poetry, he is also the founder/editor of the *Greenfield Review*. "Not a Thing of Paint or Feathers" previously appeared in *The Good Message of Handsome Lake* (Unicorn Press, 1979); "Canticle" appeared in *Flow* (Cold Mountain Press, 1975); and "From An Inmate Rule Book" appeared in *There are No Trees Inside the Prison* (Blackberry Press, 1978).

Barney Bush, Shawnee-Cayuga, was born in Saline Co., Illinois in 1946. After studying art at the Institute of American Indian Arts, he finished a degree in humanities at Ft., Lewis College in Durango, Colorado, and earned a Master's degree in English and Fine Arts from the University of Idaho. "Leaving Oklahoma Again" previously appeared in his *Petroglyphs* (Greenfield Review Press, 1982).

Ramona Carden is a member of the Colville tribe. After elementary and high school in Washington, she spent her senior year at the Institute of American Indian Arts. She received her B.A. from Eastern Washington State College. "The Moccasins of An Old Man" and "Tumbleweed" previously appeared in *The Whispering Wind*, ed. T. D. Allen, 1972.

Martha Chosa is from the Pueblo at Jemez. "Drums" previously appeared in *The South Dakota Review*.

Grey Cohoe, Navajo, was born at Shiprock, New Mexico, and attended school there and at Phoenix Indian High School. During his two years at the Institute of American Indian Arts, 1965–67, he won many awards in painting, graphics, and writing. He was granted a scholarship and studied one summer at the Haystack Mountain School of Arts, Deer Isle, Maine. Since then, he has attended the University of Arizona. Grey has been given a one-man show at the university and has been included in many exhibits in this country and in Europe. His etchings and prints are notable for their action and clarity of line. His poem, "The Folding Fan," won first place in the Fifth Annual Vincent Price Awards at the Institute.

Anita Endrezze-Danielson, Yaqui, was born in 1952 in Long Beach, California. After graduating with honors from Eastern Washington State College, she received an M.A. in creative writing from that school. Her poems have appeared in numerous magazines. "Shaman/Bear" previously appeared in The Third Woman: *Minority Writers of the United States*, ed. by Dexter Fisher (Houghton Mifflin, 1980).

Louise Erdrich was born in 1954 and grew up in Wahpeton, North Dakota. She is of German and Chippewa descent, and belongs to the Turtle Mountain Band of Chippewa. Her stories have appeared in numerous magazines, and she recently won The National Book Critics Circle Award for Best Work of Fiction of 1984 for her novel *Love Medicine*. "Jacklight," "The Lady in the Pink Mustang," and "The Strange People" appeared previously in *Jacklight* (Holt, Rinehart and Winston, 1984).

Phillip William George, after two years in Vietnam and a long year on the California desert as an Army dental technician, attended Gonzaga University and the University of California, Santa Cruz. He is a member of the Nez Perce Nation at Lapwai, Washington. He spent much of his early life with his maternal great-grandmother, living and learning the ways of his ancestors. He arrived at the Institute of American Indian Arts in the fall of 1964, a graduate of Coulee Dam High School. He was a well-known Indian dance champion of the Pacific Northwest. "Night Blessing" and "Ask The Mountains" previously appeared in *The Whispering Wind*, ed. T. D. Allen, 1972.

Janet Campbell Hale is a Coeur d'Alene, born January 11, 1947. She grew up on the Yakima and Coeur d'Alene reservations. After leaving IAIA, she went to San Francisco. She is married, has two children, and graduated with honors in 1972 from the University of California, Berkeley, where she also earned her Master's degree in journalism the following year. She taught in the Department of Native American Studies for a time, and later worked as an editorial assistant for Harcourt Brace Jovanovich. "Tribal Cemetery" was published here for the first time, but later appeared in her first volume of poetry published by Greenfield Review Press, *Custer Lives in Himbolt Country*.

Ioy Harjo, Creek, was born in Tulsa, Oklahoma, in 1951. After attending high school at the Institute of American Indian Arts, she received her B.A. from the University of New Mexico, and her M.F.A. from the Iowa Writers Workshop. She has taught Native American Literature and Creative Writing at IAIA and Arizona State University. Author of three collections of poetry, she currently lives in Santa Fe, New Mexico. "Are You Still There" previously appeared in *The Last Song* (Puerto Del Sol, 1975); "The Woman Hanging from the Thirteenth Floor Window" previously appeared in *She Had Some Horses* (Thunder's Mouth Press, 1983).

Patty Harjo is Seneca-Seminole, was born December 29, 1947 in Miami, Oklahoma, and studied at the Institute of American Arts. "Musings" previously appeared in *The South Dakota Review*.

Lance Henson, a Cheyenne from Calumet, Oklahoma, was born in 1944. He is an ex-Marine, a member of the Cheyenne Dog Soldier Warrior Society, and the Native American Church. He earned a Master's degree in creative writing from the University of Tulsa, and he is the author of several volumes of poetry. "Warrior Nation Trilogy" previously appeared in his *Naming the Dark: Poems for the Cheyenne* (Point Riders Press, 1976); "Eight Poems for August" appeared in *Mistah* (Strawberry Press, 1977).

Linda Hogan, Chickasaw, was born in Denver, Colorado, in 1947 and grew up in Oklahoma. "Celebration: Birth of a Colt" previously appeared in *Calling Myself Home* (Greenfield Review Press, 1978).

Bruce Ignacio was born on the Utah and Duray Reservation in Ft. Duchene, Utah. He attended the Institute of American Indian Arts for three years where he majored in creative writing and jewelry. He exhibited jewelry at the Scottsdale Indian Arts Exhibit in 1971 where he won first prize for his work. He is presently employed in Ft. Duchene, Utah. "Lost" previously appeared in *The South Dakota Review*.

Maurice Kenny is a Mohawk, born in 1929 in Watertown, New York. Formerly poetry editor of *Akwesasne Notes*, he is co-editor of Contact II and publisher of Strawberry Press. Author of several volumes of poetry, he is also widely published in numerous journals. "Wild Strawberry" and "Corn-Planter" previously appeared in *Dancing Back Strong the Nation* (Blue Cloud Quarterly Press, 1979); "Corn-Planter" previously appeared in *The Smell of Slaughter* (White Pine Press, 1981).

King D. Kuka was born in Browning, Montana. A member of the Blackfeet tribe, he attended high school in Valier, Montana. In 1963 he transferred to the Institute of American Indian Arts, where he studied painting, sculpture, and creative writing. He has won recognition for both his poetry and paintings and sculptures. He is currently attending the University of Montana. "A Taste of Honey" previously appeared in *The Whispering Wind*, ed. T. D. Allen 1972.

Harold Littlebird is a full-blooded Indian of Santo Domingo and Laguna tribal descent. Born in Albuquerque, New Mexico, he attended public schools in California and Utah. From grades nine through twelve he was a student at the Institute of American Indian Arts, from which he was graduated in 1969. "Death in the Woods" previously appeared in *The American Indian Speaks* (Dakota Press: U. of South Dakota, 1969).

Charles C. Long. "Yei-ie's Child" previously appeared in *The Writer's Reader*, ed. T. D. Allen (Institute of American Indian Arts, Santa Fe, New Mexico.)

Alonzo Lopez, Papago, was born in Pima County, Arizona, and attended Sells Consolidated School before entering the Institute of American Indian Arts as a sophomore. He was accepted for an interim year at Yale University when he left the Institute. He successfully completed his work at Yale and was admitted for regular college work, but he elected to transfer to Wesleyan University because curriculum offerings in American Indian Studies at Wesleyan included the Navajo language and other subjects that he desired. "Direction" and "I am Crying from Thirst" previously appeared in *The South Dakota Review*; "The Lavender Kitten" previously appeared in *The Whispering Wind*, ed. T. D. Allen, 1972.

David Martinez. "New Way, Old Way," and "This is Today" both previously appeared in *Anthology of Poetry and Verse* by American Indian Art Students (Department of Interior, BIA).

Emerson Blackhorse Mitchell was born in a hogan. He attended school at Ignacio, Colorado, until his junior year in high school when he transferred to the Institute of American Indian Arts. His father had died in service in World War II. His maternal grandparents cared for him and gave him his early training in the Navajo way. Barney attended Fort Lewis College, Durango, Colorado, for one year and transferred to Navajo Community College, Many Farms, Arizona. He is now teaching Social Science at the Round Rock School. "I'm really teaching Navajo culture," he says, and he is teaching in the Navajo language which he enjoys. "Miracle Hill" and "The New Direction" previously appeared in *The South Dakota Review*.

N. Scott Momaday is the son of a Kiowa father and Cherokee mother. Besides Vine Deloria, Jr., Momaday is probably the most widely read Indian author. He won the Pulitzer prize in 1969 for his widely acclaimed novel, *House Made of Dawn*. He also published *The way to Rainy Mountain* in 1969. He holds his Ph.D. from Stanford and is currently a professor in the English department at Stanford University. "Angle of Geese" appeared previously in *Southern Review*; the others printed in this volume all appeared previously in the *New Mexico Quarterly*.

Duane Niatum has written four volumes of poetry. *Songs for the Harvester of Dreams* (Univ. of Washington Press, 1981) won an American Book Award from the Before Columbus Foundation in 1982. In June, 1983 he was an invited participant in Rotterdam's International Poetry Festival. He edited a Harper & Row anthology, *Carriers of The Dream Wheel* (1975), which has become among the most widely read and known books on contemporary Native American poetry. He is presently working on a new anthology for Harper & Row. Niatum was born and lives in Seattle, Washington. He is of mixed-blood and a member of the Klallam Nation of Washington State. It is a Salishan tribe of salmon fishermen. The name means "strong people." His most recent teaching job was at the University of Washington in the winter of 1985. He has also published short fiction and essays. His work has been translated into many languages, including Dutch, Italian and Russian.

Calvin O'John, Ute-Navajo, was born in Denver, Colorado. He attended elementary school in Colorado before going to the Institute of American Indian Arts, where he was graduated in 1967. Besides being a poet, he is a widely exhibited painter, lauded by such authorities as the Curator of the Museum of Modern Art, N. Y. "Dancing teepees" previously appeared in *The Whispering Wind*, ed. T. D. Allen, 1972.

Simon Ortiz is of the Acoma Pueblo in New Mexico, and he is editor of the Navajo *Rough Rock News*. He spent a year studying at the University of Iowa in the International Writing Program. "Ten O'Clock News," "This Preparation" and "Smoking My Prayers" appeared previously in *The South Dakota Review*; "Relocation" appeared in *The Way: Anthology of American Indian Literature* (Vintage Books, 1972).

Agnes Pratt, Suquamish, was born at Bremerton, Washington. She attended North Kitsap Elementary School at Pousbo, Washington, and three different high schools: North Kitsap; St. Euphrasia High, Seattle Washington; and the Institute of American Indian Arts Santa Fe, New Mexico. She stayed on at the Institute for two years of graduate work. "Death Takes Only a Minute" and "Empathy" previously appeared in *Literary Cavalcade*, 1969.

Fred Red Cloud, a Denver businessman, is Seneca by descent. He is one of the editors of *The Mustang Review*, a semi-annual poetry magazine. "A Tale of Last Stands" appeared previously in *Prairie Schooner*, 1970; "Machu Picchu, Peru" appeared in *Epoch*, 1971.

Carter Revard, Osage on his father's side, was born in Pawhuska, Oklahoma, in 1931. He earned degrees from the University of Tulsa, Oxford (on a Rhodes Scholarship), and Yale. He presently teaches at Washington University in St.

Louis. His poems have appeared in numerous magazines and anthologies. "The Coyote" and "On the Bright Side" previously appeared in his *Ponca War Dancers* (Point Riders Press, 1980).

Ronald Rodgers was born at the Indian Hospital in Claremore, Oklahoma. He is a member of the Cherokee Nation. At fifteen, he entered the Institute of American Indian Arts as a sophomore. His major interest became writing, particularly short stories. He also developed an aptitude for drama and acted several major roles in school and community performances. In his junior year at IAIA, Ron won a second place in the nationwide Scholastic Awards and his short story, "The Good Run," appeared in *Cavalcade* magazine for January, 1967. Ron attended San Francisco State College during the 1968–69 Hayakawa-hiatus year, wrote on his own one term, and transferred mid-term, 1970, to UCLA. He thereafter transferred to the University of California at Santa Cruz. "Taking Off" appeared previously in *The South Dakota Review*; "Kindergarten" previously appeared in *The Whispering Wind*, ed. T. D. Allen, 1972.

Wendy Rose was born in Oakland, California, in 1948 of Hopi-Miwok-Cornish parents. She currently teaches at the University of California at Berkeley. Author of several volumes of poetry, she also edits *The American Indian Quarterly* and was the recipient of a 1982 NEA Fellowship. "Caged Wings" previously appeared in *What Happened When the Hopi Hit New York* (Contact II Publications, 1982); "I Expected My Skin and Blood To Ripen ' previously appeared in *Academic Squaw: Reports to the World from the Ivory Tower* (Blue Cloud Quarterly Press, 1977).

Norman Russell is of Cherokee ancestry and is Vice President of Academic Affairs at Central State College, Edmund, Oklahoma. His first book of poems, *At the Zoo*, was published in 1969. "The World Has Many Places, Many Ways" and "The Eyes of the Child Do Not See Me" appeared previously in *Southwest Review*; "The Great Way of the Man" and "Clerk's Song II" appeared in the *South Dakota Review*.

Bruce Severy was born in Santa Monica, California. He did undergraduate work at Washington State University before graduating from the University of California, Long Beach. He also did graduate work there. Severy has been widely published in such journals as *Dakotah Territory*, *Prairie Schooner*, *Cafe Solo*, *Measure*, *Pinache*, *the Outsider*, and others. He is currently teaching English, Journalism and Drama at Drake High School in Drake, North Dakota.

Loyal Shegonee is from Potawatomi tribal group. "Loneliness" appeared previously in *The South Dakota Review*.

Soge Track is a Sioux-Pueblo from Taos. She was a student at the Institute of American Indian Arts. "Indian Love Letter" appeared previously in *The South Dakota Review*.

Winifred Fields Walters is part Choctaw, but says that she knows the Navajo, Zuni and Hopi much better than her own tribe. She lives in Gallup, New Mexico. "Navajo Signs" appeared previously in *The South Dakota Review*.

Archie Washburn was born at Shiprock, New Mexico. He is of Navajo ancestry. He was a student at Intermountain School in Brigham City, Utah. "Hogan" and "Unknown Smoke" appeared previously in *The South Dakota Review*.

James Welch was born on a Blackfoot reservation in Browning, Montana. His father is Blackfeet and his mother is Gros Vendre. He received his B.A. from the University of Montana. He has worked as a laborer, a forest service employee, an Indian firefighter, and a counselor for Upward Bound at the University of Montana; he now devotes full time to writing. He has published in several magazines, incuding *Poetry*, *Poetry Northwest*, the *New Yorker*, *New American Review*, *The South Dakota Review*, and has also had several works anthologized. *Riding the Earthboy, 40*, his first book of poems, was published in 1971. "One More Time" and "The Man from Washington" appeared previously in *The South Dakota Review*: "Dreaming Winter" and "Harlem, Montana" appeared in *Poetry*.

Roberta Hill Whiteman is a member of the Oneida Tribe and grew up around Oneida and Green Bay, Wisconsin. She earned a B.A. from the University of Wisconsin and an M.F.A. from the University of Montana. She currently teaches at the University of Wisconsin–Eau Claire. "Star Quilt," "Overcast Dawn," and "Variations for Two Voices" previously appeared in *Star Quilt* (Holy Cow! Press, 1984).

Donna Whitewing was born in Sutherland, Nebraska. Her father was a farm hand and migrant worker during most of her growing-up years. The family roaded from South Dakota to Nebraska. Donna attended various elementary schools in Nebraska and, on leaving St. Augustine's Indian Mission at Winnebago, received a scholarship to attend Assumption Academy, Norfolk, Nebraska. Donna continues to write as well as work in the Children's Theatre in Winnebago. "August 24, 1963" appeared previously in *The South Review*; "A Vegetable, I Will Not Be" previously appeared in *The Whispering Wind*, ed. T. D. Allen, 1972.

Ray Young Bear was born in Tama, Iowa. His tribe is Sauk and Fox. The poems printed here all appeared previously in *Pembroke Magazine*.

Biographical material for: Liz Sohappy Bahe, Ramona Carden, Grey Cohoe, Phillip William George, Patty Harjo, Bruce Ignacio, King D. Kuka, Harold Littlebird, Charles C. Long, Alonzo Lopez, David Martinez, Emerson Blackhorse Mitchell, Calvin O'John, Agnes Pratt, Ronald Rogers, Loyal Shegonee, and Dona Whitewing is used by permission of T. D. Allen and the Institute of American Indian Arts, Sante Fe, New Mexico, a Bureau of Indian Affairs School.